Use FreeMind

THOMAS ECCLESTONE

NONFICTION BOOKS BY AUTHOR

APPLICATION GUIDES
Celestia 1.6 Beginners Guide
Use Opera: The Internet Browser
Use FreeMind: MindMap Software

DOCUMENT PRODUCTION
Use Magix Photo Designer: A Beginners Guide
Use Scribus: The Desk Top Publishing Program

OFFICE PRODUCTIVITY
Use LibreOffice Writer: A Beginners Guide
Use LibreOffice Impress: A Beginners Guide
Use LibreOffice Base: A Beginners Guide
Use LibreOffice Calc: A Beginners Guide

COMPANY MANAGEMENT SOFTWARE
Use Podio: To Manage A Small Company
Use ProjectLibre: for Project Management

CONTENTS

DEDICATION

This book is dedicated to my Grandmother

1FIRST STEPS

Download FreeMind

You can download FreeMind from a number of sources. One of the best is Sourceforge. Below is the current URL download link, but you may need to google it since the direct link can change over time.

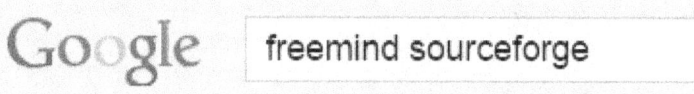

Once you click on search Google should return the download website:

FreeMind - SourceForge
freemind.sourceforge.net/ ▾
FreeMind is a premier free mind-mapping software written in Java. The recent development has hopefully turned it into high productivity tool. We are proud that ...

Download
2 Step-by-step overview; 3 Download;
4 Older versions ...

Download freemind-bin-ma...
Your download will start shortly...
Problems with the download ...

FreeMind
Download FreeMind. A premier mind-mapping software ...

Alternatives to FreeMind
To achieve that which FreeMind offers, you can use variety of ...

When you click on Download you're taken to a website with the following URL

← → C 🗋 freemind.sourceforge.net/wiki/index.php/Download#Download

I'd suggest that you install the all-inclusive version since it is very useful to be able to save to PDF. In this book I'm going to be installing the windows version, but all other versions are very similar. Whichever version you are going to install click on it.

| MS Windows | Windows Installer Max 🗗 | 38 | All-inclusive version |

You'll see a progress webpage.

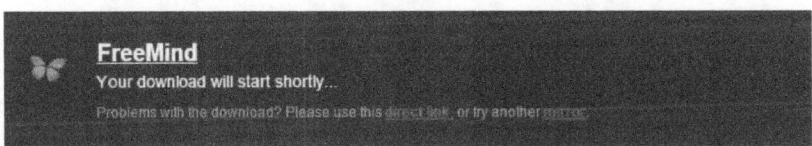

After a short while the download will start. Different browsers don't look precisely the same, but in Chrome you see the following at the bottom left hand of the screen. Obviously you'll be familiar with your own browser.

Once finished the download will look something like the following in Chrome:

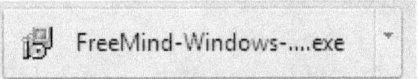

Install FreeMind

Either click on the download in chrome or go to the download folder and double click on the installer. You'll see a user account control dialogue which will ask you if you want to allow the program to make changes. Click Yes.

FreeMind will ask you what language you want to install the program in. Click on the combo box and select the language that you want from the list (often you'll find the default language is correct anyway).

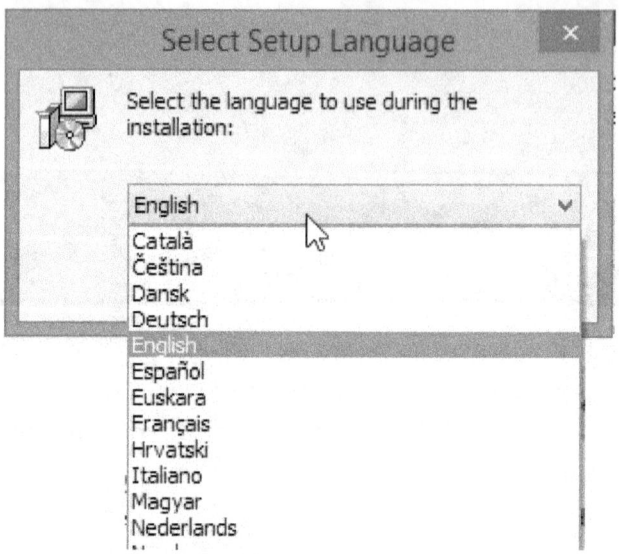

When you've selected the correct language click
OK .You'll see a welcome screen asking you to close other applications. Once you've closed anything that you have running on your computer click Next > .

The next screen provides you with a copy of the applications license. Read the license and if you agree with it click on the round circle next to ○ I accept the agreement . Then click Next > . The next screen tells you what version of Java you need. Make sure you have the right version of java and click Next > .

Verifying Java
Skip this section if you have the correct version of Java Installed.

You can verify your version of Java by going to https://www.java.com/en/download/installed.jsp in your browser. The following example is for Chrome, but other browsers are very similar.

When you load the webpage you will see a message saying verify java.

Click on the button. Java will ask permission to run:

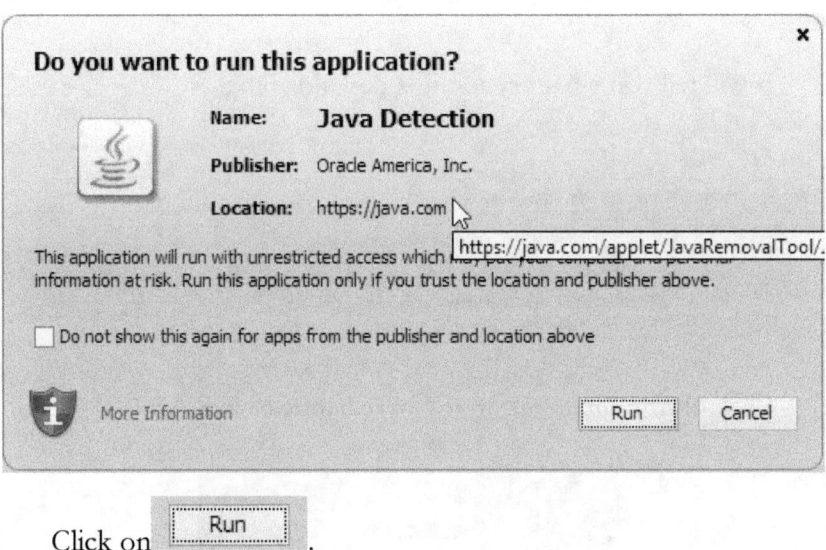

Click on ⌐Run⌐.

If Java Says the version is up to date that's all you need to do.

Your Java is Out of Date

A newer version of Java is available
Your Java version: Version 8 Update 31
Latest Java version: Version 8 Update 40

Check that the version number is adequate to run FreeMind (you found out the minimum version earlier). If it is, then you don't have to choose to install the latest version of Java which can take some time. You may choose to – but that's up to you. It's often a good idea to have the most up to date version installed.

Installing Java

If you don't have a version of Java that is new enough and you still want to install FreeMind you will need to install Java. This will take some time, so only do it when you're not going to be busy for a

while. Click on 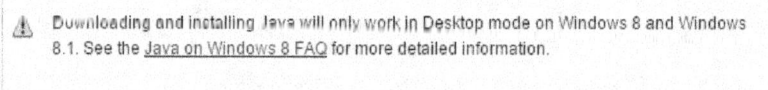 in the verification window.

It will tell you what version it is downloading:

Download Java for Windows

Recommended Version 8 Update 40 (filesize: 547 KB)

⚠ Downloading and installing Java will only work in Desktop mode on Windows 8 and Windows 8.1. See the Java on Windows 8 FAQ for more detailed information.

Click on the agree button if you're happy to install it.

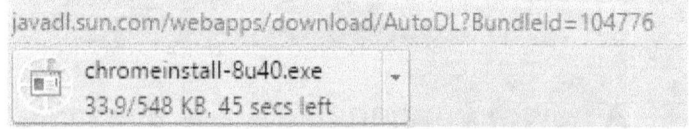

You'll see the download start.

javadl.sun.com/webapps/download/AutoDL?BundleId=104776

chromeinstall-8u40.exe
33.9/548 KB, 45 secs left

Save all files you're working on and close down all programs except your internet browser. The browser will be downloading your installer. Each browser does this in a slightly different way, so make sure you know how your browser works.

When it's finished click on it:

And agree to make changes (Pres Yes). The installer will start. Click on ___Install >___ .

The installer will start to download files that it needs. This may take some time, so it's a good idea to go and have a cup of coffee. There's an estimate for how long it'll take on the right hand side of the screen.

At this point close your Internet Browser.

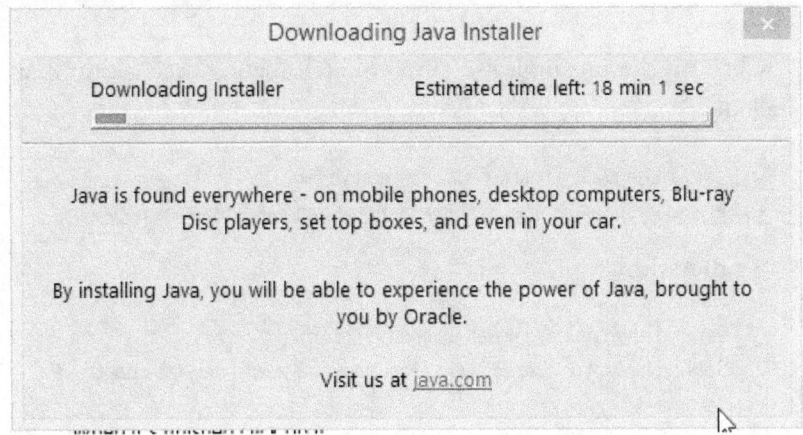

Java unfortunately sometimes tries to install some things you don't want:

Click on the rectangles to stop yourself having the Ask toolbar installed.

☑ Set and keep Ask as my default search provider
☑ Set and keep Ask.com as my browser home page and new tabs page

So they show:

☐ Set and keep Ask as my default search provider
☐ Set and keep Ask.com as my browser home page and new tabs page

Then Click Next > to continue the installation.

When it finishes it may display a confirmation dialogue. Click "OK" or "Yes". Your default browser will open to verify your Java Version:

Verify Java Version

Check to ensure that you have the recommended version of Java installed for your operating system.

 Verifying your Java version will only work in Desktop mode on Windows 8 and Windows 8.1. See the Java on Windows 8 FAQ for more detailed information.

Repeat the process above. If it's all worked successfully you should see:

Verified Java Version

 Congratulations!

You have the recommended Java installed (Version 8 Update 40).

You will need to start the FreeMind installer again. Go to the download folder and double click on the installer. You'll see a user account control dialogue which will ask you if you want to allow the program to make changes. Click Yes.

FreeMind will ask you what language you want to install the program in. Click on the combo box and select the language that you want from the list (often you'll find the default language is correct anyway).

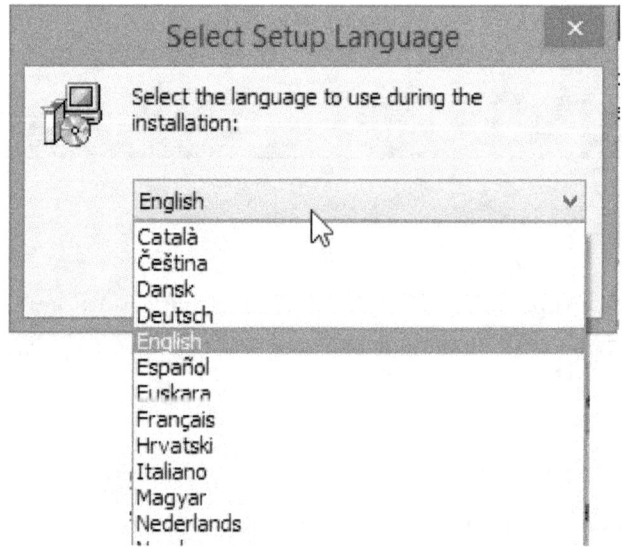

When you've selected the correct language click OK .You'll see a welcome screen asking you to close other applications. Once you've closed anything that you have running on your computer click Next > .

The next screen provides you with a copy of the applications license. Read the license and if you agree with it click on the round circle next to ◯ I accept the agreement . Then click Next > . And Next > again. This will take you back to the same position you would have been in if you had a current version of Java.

Continuing the Installation

Start the FreeMind installer again and repeat the previous steps FreeMind will tell you what directory it wants to install to. For example on my system it was:

C:\Program Files (x86)\FreeMind

Generally this directory will be OK, but you can click on Browse... to open a browse for folder dialogue. Once you've chosen your directory click Next >. I generally recommend leaving the next option, the start-up folder, as the default. Click Next > again.

You're almost there. You can decide whether to create a desktop or quick launch icon. I generally find leaving these settings toggled on is best:

Additional icons:
☑ Create a desktop icon
☑ Create a Quick Launch icon

But click the ☑ to turn these options off. I really recommend leaving ☑ Associate Freemind with the .mm file extension as it is too. Click Next > check the settings then Install. You will see a progress bar for the installer extracting files.

Extracting files...
C:\Program Files (x86)\FreeMind\plugins\script\groovy-all-1.5.6.jar

Followed by a message telling you the contributors. Click Next >. Then Finish.

You can start FreeMind by clicking on the   icon on

the desktop, or searching for it by pressing the   button or

windows key and then running a search using   and then typing
in FreeMind and clicking the icon.

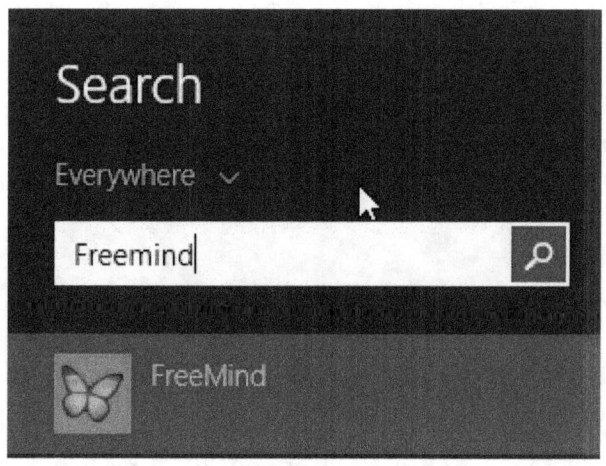

The Opening Screen

When you open FreeMind for the first time you'll see a
reasonably complex starting screen. It can help to divide these into
parts.

In the middle of the screen is the Mind Map view or main
viewable area. It contains the simplest mind map you can imagine –
the New Mind Map – when you open the screen for the first time.

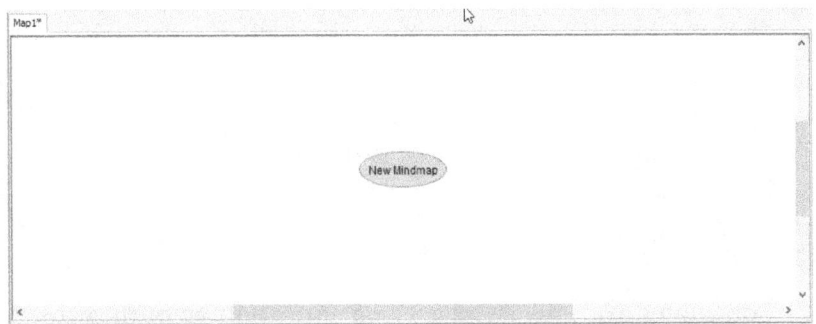

Above the Mind Map view there is a series of menu items:

File Edit View Insert Format Navigate Tools Maps Help

These allow you to control many of the features of the program, for example File allows you to save and open files, edit allows you to cut and paste nodes, and insert allows you to insert objects – often nodes – into the mind map.

Below the menu view are a number of toolbars. For example there are buttons that you can use to create, open and save files to cut copy and paste to undo and redo and so on.

I'll explain these features later in the book.

To the left of the main menu you'll see the Secondary Toolbar. These options allow you to edit nodes, add some standard graphics to the nodes, and other features that are often very useful when you want to produce a mind map.

Sometimes, you may also see a box at the bottom of the screen called the Note Window. This note window allows you to add text about the Mind Map node.

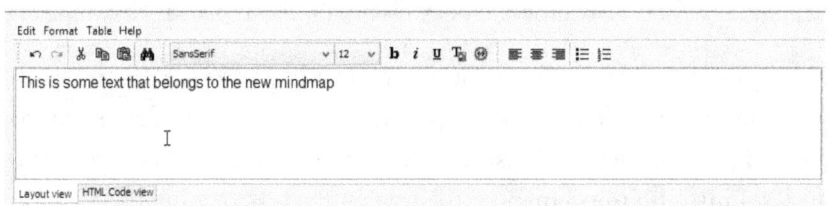

While Mind Maps are often used to create a visual display of information, it's also the case that they can also be used to outline research, projects, and break down problems. The Note View will allow you to use text to illustrate what a node means.

Note that you can also include tables with the text in the Note Window.

Creating a Simple Mind Map

Now that you've seen the opening screen of FreeMind you will want to get stuck in. The first Mind Map that we're going to create will be fairly simple but it will also teach you most of the features that you will use day in and day out.

Editing the Root Node

The first step when using FreeMind is to edit the root node so that it describes the Mind Map that you're going to produce. The Root Node is at the centre of the Mind Map by default. When you start it is called "New Mind map".

Double Click on it. You'll see a Text Box open up. Once you click at any point within the text you can edit it.

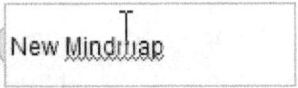

At this stage I'm going to be creating a Mind Map called Coffee. Type in the text and then press enter.

Note that a node is like a concept, task, or area. In other words, the root node is the main thing that the diagram is about. On its own that isn't very useful. Fortunately you can break the diagram down into more basic concepts.

Creating Sub nodes

A sub node is very similar to a root node. In fact, you can think of each sub node as a root node of a new Mind Map, rather like a branch of a tree spawns other branches. To create a new child note right click on the root node and then select

💡 New Child Node	Insert

.

As you can see above the root node becomes a text box which you can then type new text into. For example "How to make".

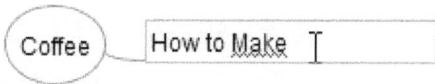

When you type enter the new node will appear. One of the things that you'll notice is that the new child node is highlighted, and the root node isn't.

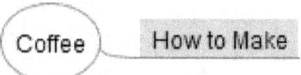

When you create a child node it is automatically selected. To select another node (or child node) in the diagram, click on it. This can be quite important later on when you're using buttons to add times, icons, or annotate nodes. FreeMind will automatically edit the selected node. So always keep an eye on what node has been selected.

Now, we've created a very simple mind map with just one child node. You can break the root node down further into other concepts by clicking on it so that it is selected.

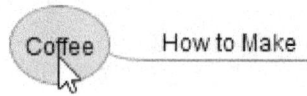

Then right clicking on it, and then clicking

on 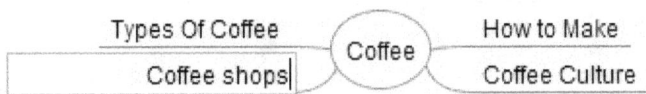. You then type in the content that you want for that node. It's possible to do this as many times as you want.

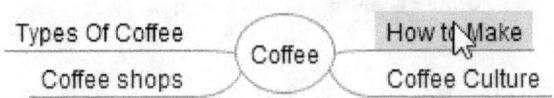

Further breaking down Child Nodes

So far we've produced a mind map with just one "Level". In effect we've got the main subject areas of the Mind Map but each of them are still quite vague. Each child node can be the root for a further set of child nodes.

Click on a child node that you want to break down further. This will select the ChildNode.

You can then either right click and choose 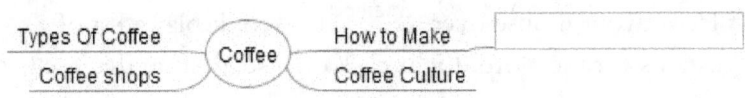 or look at the top of the screen in the toolbar. You'll see a new child node button ⊽ . If you click on the new child node button you'll see that you're inserting a new node into the diagram:

Type in the name of the node, and repeat the process,

remembering to select the node which you want to break down before inserting at each step.

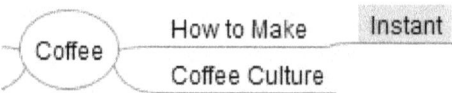

Spell checking when you are creating nodes

Everyone's human and everyone sometimes makes a spelling mistake. By default FreeMind always checks your spelling when you're editing a node. Say, you make a bit of a blunder. Espresso definitely isn't spelled like this!

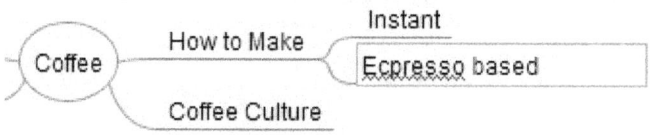

FreeMind catches the error, underlining it in red. If you right click on the underlined word, you'll see two options. The First is Spelling, which gives you suggestions of other spellings for the word.

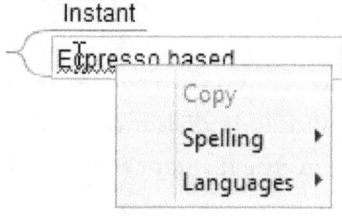

Hover your mouse over Spelling ▸ to display a list of suggestions for the word. Right click on a suggestion that contains the right spelling for the word.

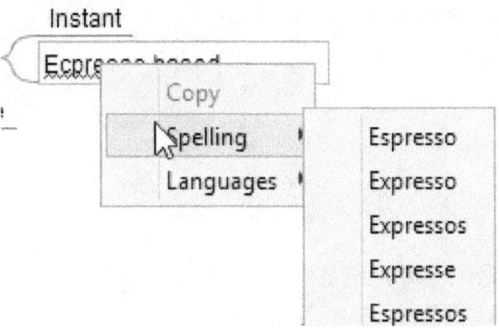

Sometimes you may be using a word that isn't actually in your default language (English, for most people who are reading this book!) to choose a foreign language hover your mouse over Languages ▸ and select it from the list.

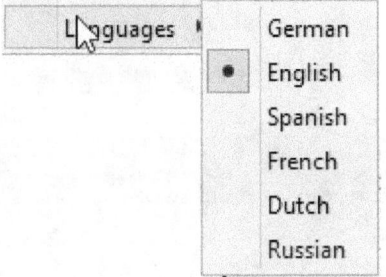

Hiding Sub Nodes

While you will often break down a diagram into child nodes the amount of detail that this gives you can often be too large. Diagrams can become unwieldy, and you may not want to break it down any further than necessary for your particular purpose.

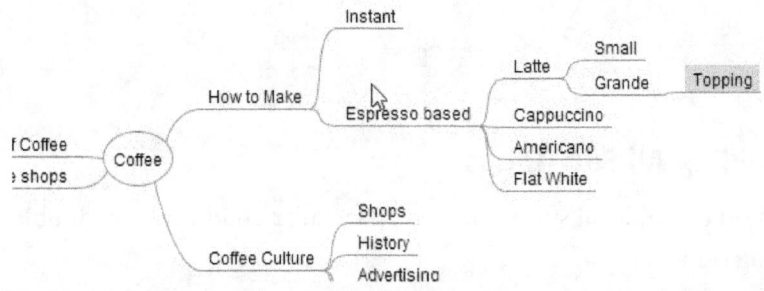

Each node has a level assigned to it. For example, the root node can be thought of as level 0

Child Nodes off the root node can be thought of as level one:

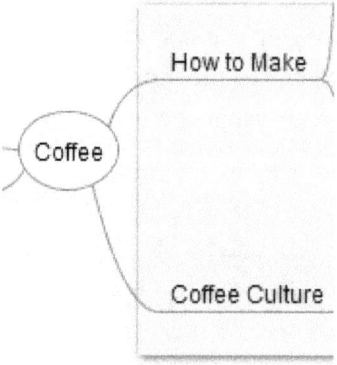

And their child nodes as level two:

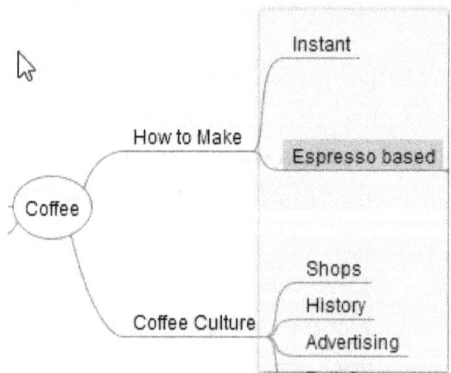

Hiding All Sub nodes

You can hide all sub nodes of a particular child node by double clicking on it:

Note that when you've hidden child nodes you'll see a little round circle at the end of the node:°.

Click on a node with ° at the end to see display all child nodes from that subnode.

Hiding a layer

When you want to hide a layer of nodes, select your branch node first by single clicking on it:

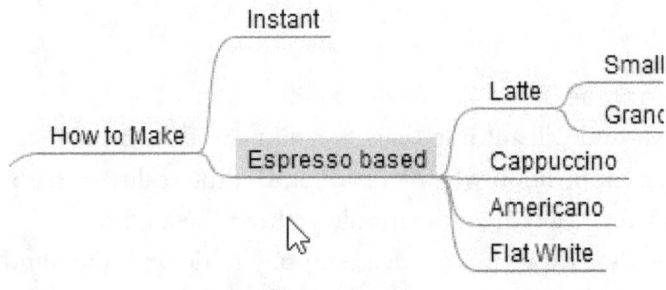

And then in the toolbar click on fold one level ⊖.

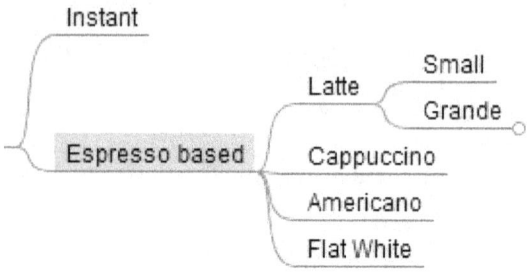

You can repeat the process to fold another level by clicking on 🗖 again.

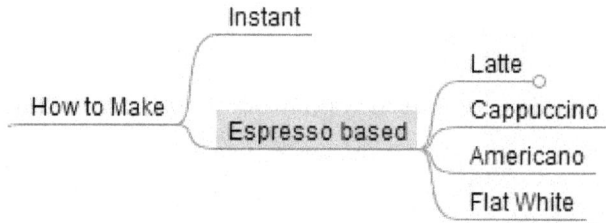

You can show (or unfold) a layer by selecting the branch node as above, and then clicking on unfold one level ➕.

Moving a Node

FreeMind will automatically position a node to what it considers the optimum position when you add it. But the reality is that it positions the diagram automatically without the kind of understanding of what you are attempting to do with the mind map. So you'll often find that it is necessary to move a node in the mind map.

If you go to the point that the node connects to its child objects you'll see a large round circle:

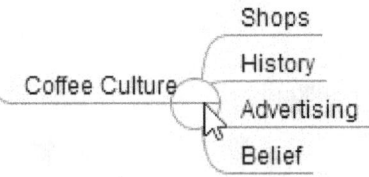

Slowly move closer to the text of the node that you want to move. When you get to the correct position you'll see an ellipse. The mouse button will also change until it is a compass.

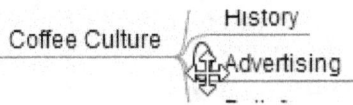

Click and hold the mouse, then move the mouse to the position where you want the node.

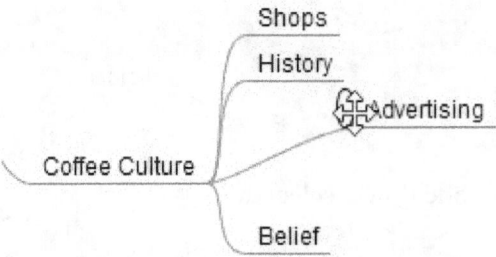

You'll see that the node changes location. One thing you will find, though is that the order of the node won't change. In other words, if you move Advertising upwards in the above diagram you'll also see History and Shops moving to make way for the change.

Node Up and Node Down

The above problem is relatively easy to fix. First, select the node that you want to move up (i.e. above another node).

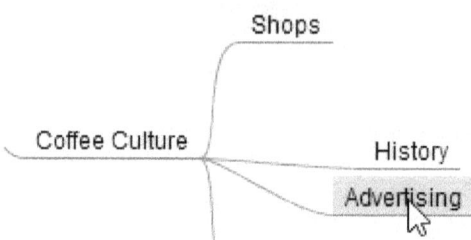

Then in the Navigate menu click on Node Up   Ctrl+Up   . You will see that History and Advertising are swapped. FreeMind automatically calculates the best placement for these nodes so you may have to move them manually.

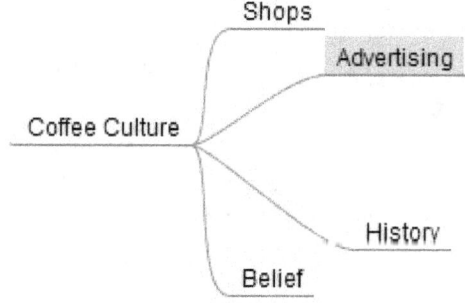

To move a node down, select it.

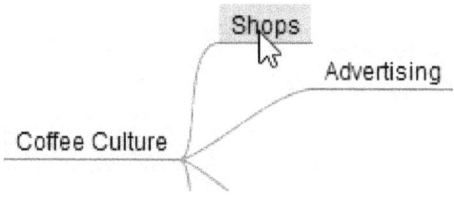

And then click on Node Down   Ctrl+Down in the Navigate menu. You will sometimes find that the automatic placement of the nodes is a bit weird when you move objects up or down. You can solve this problem by moving them manually.

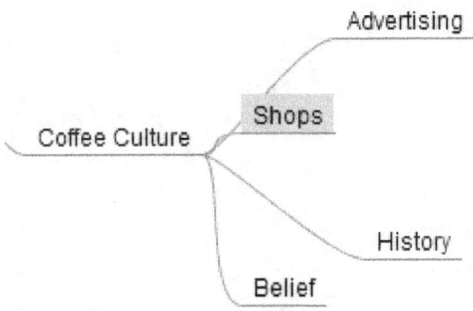

Moving a Node to the left or right

In the same way that you can move a node up or down you can also move it to the left or right. First select the node that you want to move to the left.

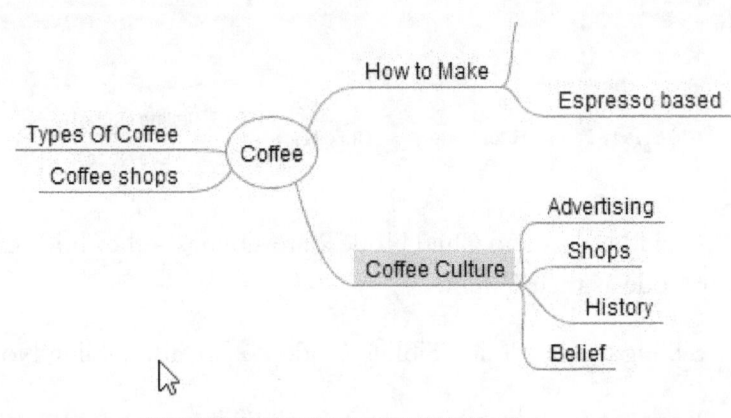

Then click on Node Left   Ctrl+Left   in the Navigate menu to move it to the left.

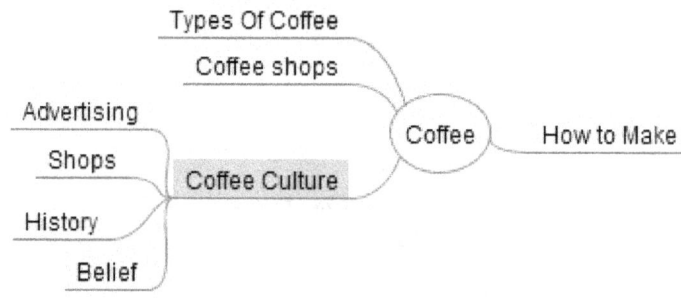

Obviously you'll need to move it up or down if you want it to switch places. You can use  Node Right   Ctrl+Right in the Navigate menu to move the Node to the right.

More on inserting Nodes

We've already covered the concept of Child Nodes and Root or Parent Nodes. Sibling Nodes have the same parent node as each other.

Child Node 1 and Child Node 2 are siblings – they both have Root Node as their Parent.

Sibling Node 1-1 and Sibling Node 1-2 are also Sibling Nodes.

Root Node and Child Node 2 aren't Sibling nodes – their relationships is Parent Node and Child Node.

Child Node 2 and Sibling Node 1-1 aren't Sibling nodes – they aren't on the same branch.

When you add a new Sibling Node it has an order associated with it. We've already showed you how to change the order (i.e. move a node to the left or right or up or down) but it can be convenient to add a sibling node before the current one, or after it. To add a new Sibling node after the current node click on

New Sibling Node   Enter   in the Insert menu:

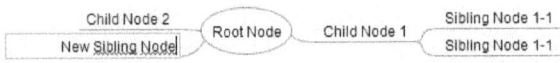

To insert a sibling node before the current node click
New Previous Sibling Node   Shift+Enter in the Insert Menu. (I.e. we've selected New Sibling Node and click New Previous Sibling Node   Shift+Enter):

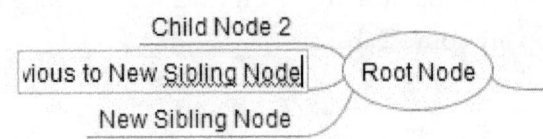

New Parent Node

Sometimes you may want to insert a new parent node between the currently selected node and its' parent. Click on

New Parent Node   Shift+Insert to do this. For example if we select Previous to New Sibling Node and insert a New Parent Node we get):

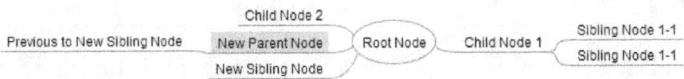

Making a New Diagram

To create a new Mind Map click on 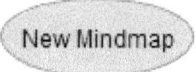. You'll see a new Mind Map in the viewable area:

New Mindmap

Toggling between Open Mind Maps

You might be concerned that you've lost the existing Mind Map. Don't be. FreeMind can edit several different Mind Maps at the same time. You'll see that just above the area where you're editing the Mind Map are some Tabs:

Map2* Map3*

There are two tabs open here (you might have Map1 and Map2. Every time you create a new Mind Map, the number at the end increases by one). The other thing you'll see is the asterisk * at the end of the filename. This means that you haven't saved the diagram yet.

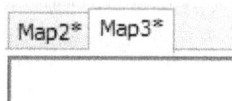

To go to the earlier map, click on it in the file tabs bar.

You'll see the Mind Map view change to display the file that you were editing earlier.

Navigating to Other Mind Maps

Say you have the following files open:

| New Mindmap.mm | Coffee.mm | How to Make.mm | Types Of Coffee.mm* | Development.mm |

Obviously you're editing Coffee at the moment. You can either click on a file on the tab or use

Previous Map   Ctrl+Page Up   in the Maps menu to move to the map on the left of the toolbar:

| New Mindmap.mm | Coffee.mm | How to Make.mm | Types Of Coffee.mm* | Development.mm |

Note that if you're in the first file in the tab and use

Previous Map   Ctrl+Page Up   you circle round and open the last file.

| New Mindmap.mm | Coffee.mm | How to Make.mm | Types Of Coffee.mm* | Development.mm |

You can also use   Next Map   Ctrl+Page Down   . in the Maps menu to move to the map on the right.

Why is this useful? Well, note the text on the right   Previous Map   Ctrl+Page Up . This is a shortcut. Wherever I tell you click on an option in a menu and you see a keyboard shortcut you can also use a keyboard combo to carry out the required action. For example, you can hold the control key and press the Page Up key on the keyboard to move to the previous map.

This can save a lot of time.

Moving Mind Map to Left or Right

Sometimes you may want to move a mind map to the left or right in the File Tab. First, open the correct file by clicking on it or navigating to it.

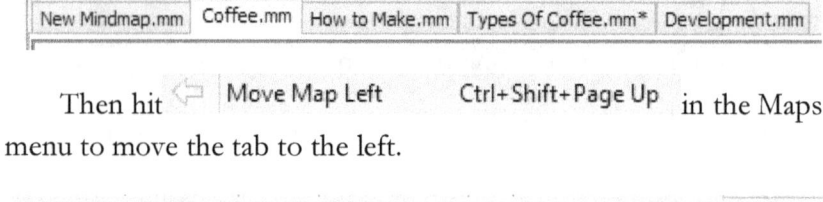

Then hit 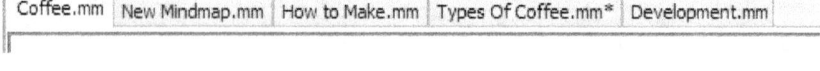 in the Maps menu to move the tab to the left.

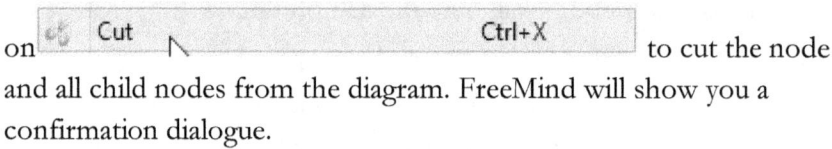

Or ⇨ Move Map Right Ctrl+Shift+Page Down to move it to the right of the file tab.

Cut, Copy and Paste Nodes

Sometimes you may want to move nodes around the diagram. One of the easiest ways to do this is to cut, copy or paste nodes. You can also use this to move nodes between different diagrams. The difference between cut and copy is that if you cut a node it will disappear and be stored in memory, if you copy a node it won't be deleted but a copy will be stored in memory.

To Cut

The first step is to right click on the Node that you want to cut. You'll see a context sensitive menu appear. Click on ✂ Cut   Ctrl+X to cut the node and all child nodes from the diagram. FreeMind will show you a confirmation dialogue.

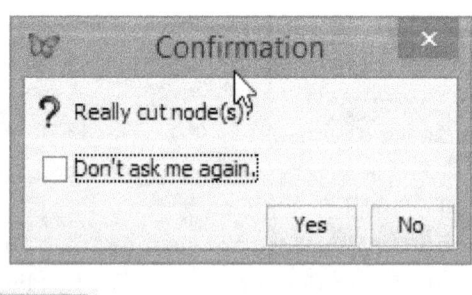

Click on Yes to confirm the steps.

You'll see that the Node and all sub nodes (i.e. nodes on a lower level) will be removed from the diagram. Don't worry! It's stored in memory so you will be able to recover it.

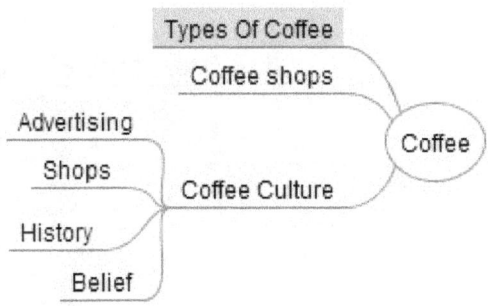

To Paste

The first step is to select the node where you want to paste the content of the clipboard. The node you've cut or copied will be pasted as a sub node of the one that you've selected. It's possible to paste to any node including the Root Node.

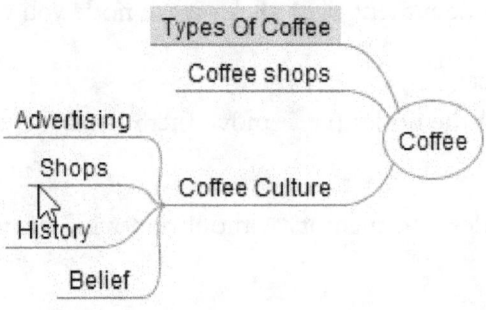

Then, click on in the edit menu. (You can also right click on any node and select paste from the context sensitive menu). You'll see that the item that you've copied will appear below the location you selected earlier.

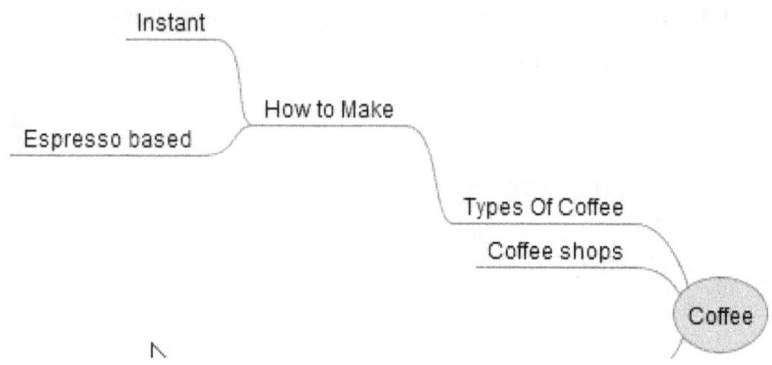

To copy

You can copy a node by right clicking on it and selecting Copy   Ctrl+C from the context sensitive menu.

Paste into another Mind Map

We showed you earlier that it's possible to edit two or more documents at the same time using the file tab. If you want to move nodes to a new document right click on the node you want to move and either select Cut   Ctrl+X if you want to cut the nodes (i.e. remove them from the original document) or Copy   Ctrl+C if you want to copy the nodes into memory without removing them from the map.

Then in the File Tab click on the document that you want to paste to Map2* Map3*. In this case it's the New Mind map we edited earlier although it will differ depending on what files you have open. Select the node you want to paste to as normal.

And click on <img src="paste" /> **Paste** Ctrl+V to paste it into the document.

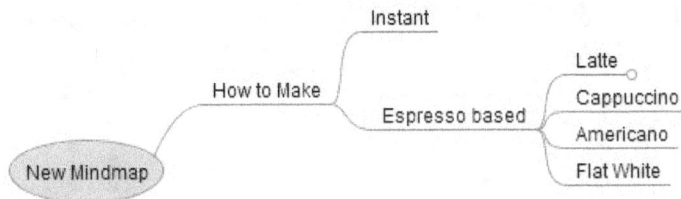

Undo and Redo

When you make a mistake in FreeMind you can make use of the single-step undo facility by clicking on ✎. This undoes one step at a time. You can change your mind and Redo a step by clicking on ↷.

There's unfortunately no multi-step undo facility so it is a case of undoing one step at a time. If you're about to do a lot of changes that you're not sure about saving the file and then reverting it (see later on in this chapter) can be a good idea.

Changing Root Node

The above diagram is wonky. We've got what's obviously the real root node <u>How to Make</u> as a subordinate of a root node that doesn't make sense.

You can't delete New Mind Map until you've made <u>How to Make</u> the root node. To do this, select the node that you want to make into the root node:

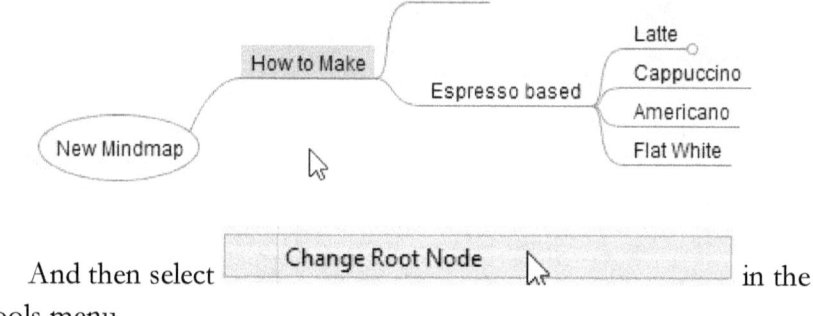

And then select 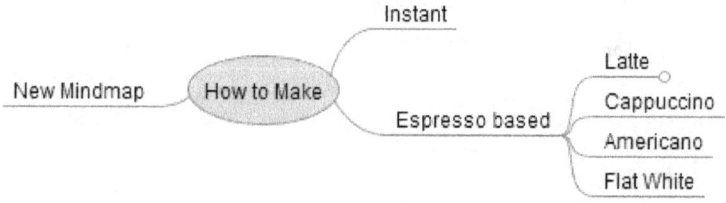 in the Tools menu.

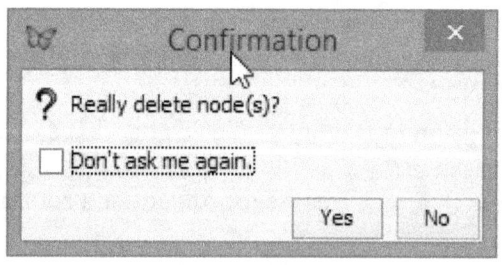

Deleting a Node

You can delete a node by right clicking on it and

selecting ☒ Remove Node   Delete from the context sensitive menu. You will see a prompt to ask you if you are sure.

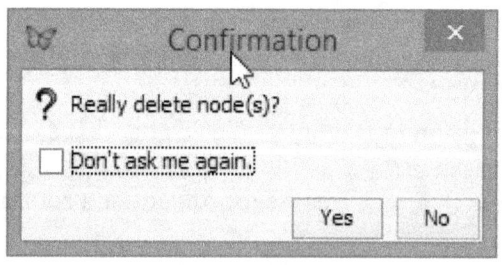

Click on Yes to confirm that you want to remove the node. If you remove a node you'll also remove any child nodes.

Adding Annotations to Nodes (the Note Window)

Often you'll want to add notes to a node. You can do this

through the Note Window which is sometimes below the Mind Map view.

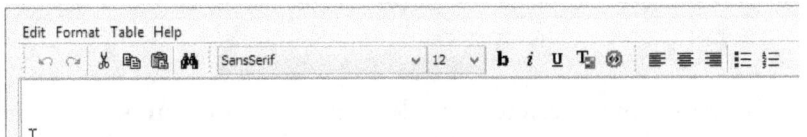

If you can't see the above window, check in the view window. You'll see a Note Window Option.

Click on it to toggle the window on. You'll see the Note Window appear, and if you check the View menu you'll see a rectangle that shows that the Note Window has been toggled on.

You can click on it again to turn it off once you're done with it.

In the Note Window you can type in information about the Node. I'll describe how to use it in more detail later.

For the moment select a node and enter in text into the window.

When you click onto another node, FreeMind will put a symbol by the one you've just annotated:

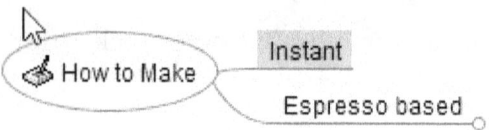

Because you've selected a node without an annotation, the Note Window will be empty. But if you click back onto the node you've just added a note to you'll see it appear in the window.

At first these Annotations may not appear all that useful. However, when you export a diagram they will appear as part of the document. For example, if I export as .odt format when I open it in LibreOffice it shows the following outline:

How to Make

This is how to make a coffee

1 Instant

2 Espresso based

- Latte
  - Small
  - Grande
    - Topping
- Cappuccino
- Americano
- Flat White

I will explain how to export documents later on.

Save Mind Map

To save a mind map click on in the toolbar. Note that if the file hasn't already been saved it will open a Save As dialogue. Choose the directory in the normal way.

Also choose the File Name

File name: Coffee.mm

And select Save .

You can see in the File Tab that a file has been edited since the last time it was saved because there will be an asterisk (star) by the name. When a file has already been given a name, clicking on will save it without a Save As dialogue. Instead, you'll see that the asterisk disappears from the File Tab.

Save As

When you want to give a file a new name (for example, when you want to save it as a new version) click on to open a Save As dialogue.

Save All

Sometimes you may have a lot of files that you've changed all open at the same time.

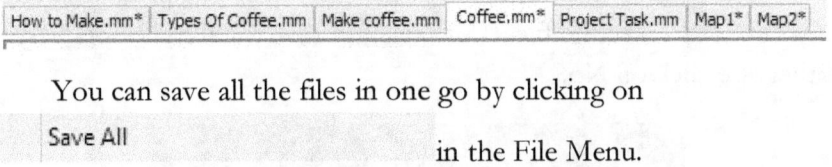

You can save all the files in one go by clicking on

Save All

in the File Menu.

If you have Maps that you haven't already saved, it will open a Save As dialogue for each map in turn so you'll be able to give them names.

Open Mind Map

To Open an existing Mind Map file click on in the Tools menu. This will display a File Open dialogue. You can use this in the normal way, choosing your directory first.

Then you can double click on the Mind Map that you want to open.

Close Mind Map

First, click on the Mind Map that you want to close in the File Tabs if you're not editing it already.

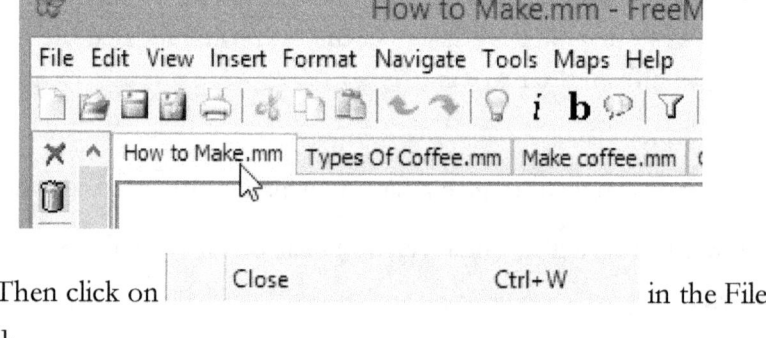

Then click on Close Ctrl+W in the File Menu.

If you've already saved the Mind Map you'll just see that the file close, and go to the next open file in the File Tab. If you haven't saved the Mind Map since making changes you'll see a prompt asking if you want to save the file. If you want to save the file click on Yes, otherwise click on No.

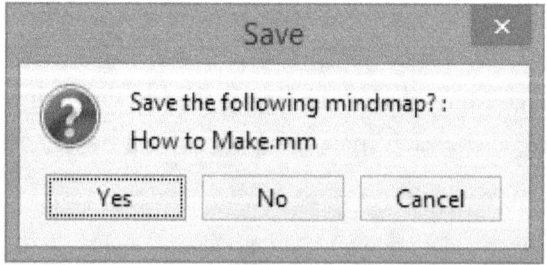

If you haven't already saved the Mind Map then FreeMind will open a SaveAs dialogue which will prompt you for a FileName and Folder.

Revert File

WARNING: WHEN YOU REVERT A FILE YOU LOSE ALL CHANGES THAT YOU HAVE MADE SINCE THE LAST SAVE

Sometimes you may edit a file and decide that you just don't like all the changes you've made. You can revert a file to the same status as it was when you last saved it by making sure you're editing the right file in the file tabs:

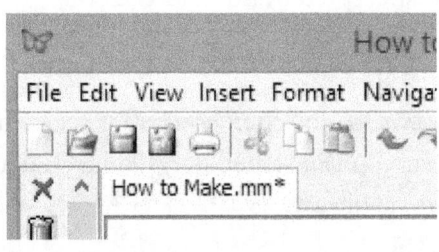

And then clicking on Revert in the File Menu.

Most Recent Files

To see the files you've saved most recently hover your mouse over Most Recent Files in the File menu to see a list of files:

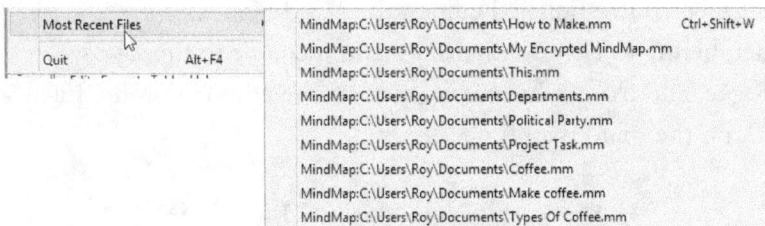

If you click on a file in the list you'll open the file. Note, if the file is Open already selecting it from the list has the same effect as clicking on the File Name in the File Tabs. Or, in other words, it doesn't revert the file to how it was when you opened the file or open up a second copy.

Encrypted Mind Map

While not exactly the same security level 007 (Licensed to Mind Map) would have used FreeMind does provide the ability to encrypt and password protect a Mind Map. This can be useful when you want to make sure that only authorised people can open and read the document.

Create the Encrypted Mind Map

To create an Encrypted Mind Map click on 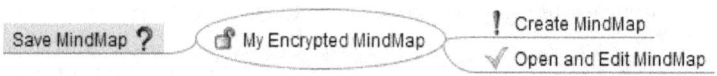 in the File Menu.

Enter the password, and then confirm it again. It's important to use a password that you can remember. One technique for doing that is to use a memorable phrase.

Note that you can edit the Mind Map in the normal way, adding nodes, icons, and formatting.

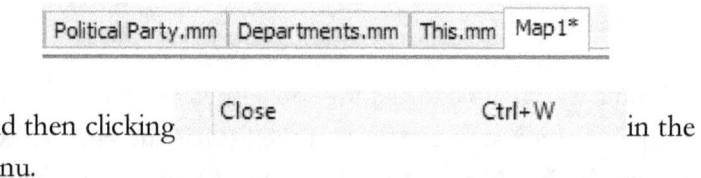

Once you've finished editing the Mind Map save it ⌷, remembering to choose the folder and filename in the save as dialogue, and close it by making sure you're editing it in the File Tabs (click on the mind map if necessary)

| Political Party.mm | Departments.mm | This.mm | Map 1* |

And then clicking Close   Ctrl+W in the File Menu.

Why are we closing the mind map? When you create a mind map by default the Encryption is toggled off. I.e. you'll see an open padlock  by the mind map and you'll be able to edit and see the mind map.

Toggle Encryption on or Off

When you open the Mind Map after saving it, the Encryption will be toggled on. Remember, to open a file click on

🖼 Open...   Ctrl+O   in the File menu and then select the file in the Open dialogue.

The newly open mind map will look like this:

🔒 My Encrypted MindMap

You'll not be able to edit it! To toggle the encryption off click on

🔓 Toggle Crypted / Encrypted   in the Insert Menu. FreeMind will prompt you to enter a password.

Type it in, and then press ⬚OK⬚ . If you have the right password you will be able to edit the mind map. If not, it will warn you. When you press OK you'll have to try to enter the password

again.

There's no way to recover an encrypted mind map if you forget the password. So don't do that!

Insert Encrypted Nodes

Just because you've got an Open Mind Map doesn't mean that the encrypted fun necessarily ends. It's possible to insert an Encrypted Node into a mind map that isn't password protected.

Select the parent node, and then instead of inserting a child node using ♀ click on 🔒 Insert Encrypted Node... in the insert menu.

Add a Password to the node.

You'll see the new Encrypted node. It's unlocked at the

moment.

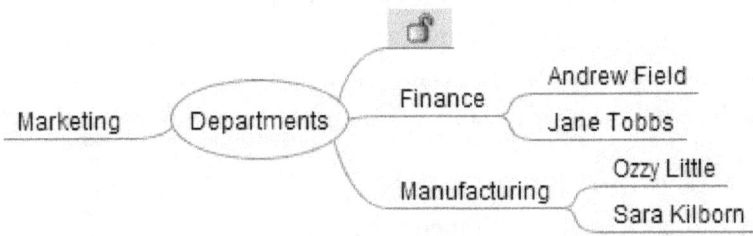

Edit the Node In the normal way.

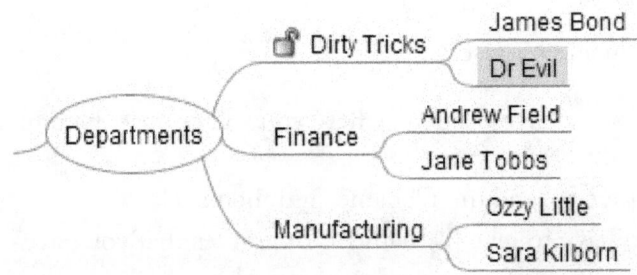

To toggle the nodes encryption on first select the node and then click 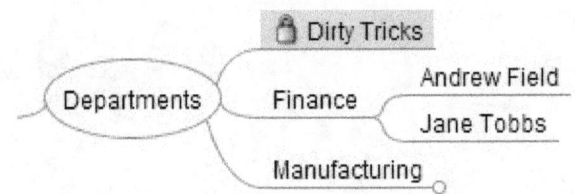 in the Insert Menu.

To toggle it back off, select the node and click Toggle Crypted / Encrypted again.

Exporting an Branch

The above example where I used Cut and Paste to create a new mind map from an existing branch was very cumbersome. While the method I used works I used it to display how to use cut, copy and paste rather than using it because it's the best way to approach the problem.

Instead, exporting the Branch is easier.

First, right click on the Branch to export. Hover your mouse over ⌐ Export   ▸⌐ in the Context Sensitive menu and choose ⌐ Branch As New Mind   Alt+Shift+A ⌐.

You will see a Save dialogue where you will choose the directory you want to save to, and the filename, and then click ⌐ Save ⌐. You may also have to give file name to other files that you have opened if you haven't saved them already.

Once you've done this you'll see the new Mind Map.

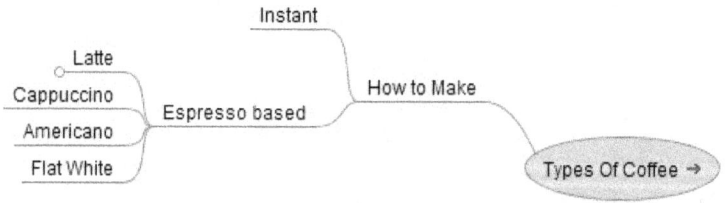

An interesting feature you haven't come across yet is the link symbol in the root node →. When you hover your mouse over a node with the link symbol the mouse will change to a hand pointer.

Clicking on the link will open the file. If it's a mind map it'll open in FreeMind. I'll describe other types of links latter in the book.

Export your Mind Map

We've covered the basic concept of exporting a branch of a mind map to a new file above. But it's also possible to export a Mind Map into other formats such as pictures (PNG or JPEG) as a clickable web page (HTML or XHTML) as a flash applet or Open Office (.odt) file.

To see a full list of the file types that you can export to hover your mouse over Export ▶ in the File menu.

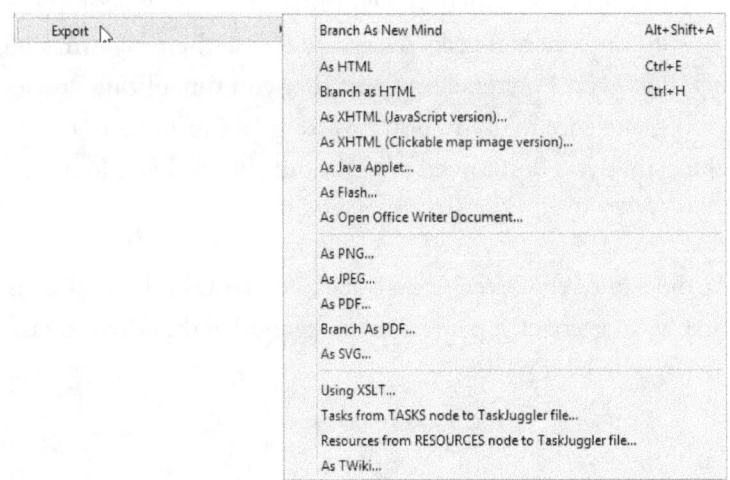

There are two main types of export. Branch exports (Branch as New Mind, Branch as HTML etc.) will export only the current branch to a file of the type described. I.e. Branch as New Mind will export the current branch to a new mind map.

The second type is AS, which exports the entire mind map to a file of the specified format, for example AS Jpeg exports it as a JPEG file.

The procedure for most of the Branch Exports is to select the node whose branch you want to export, then select the file type in the Export List, choose a directory to save to and a file name and click OK.

For the As Exports you simply select the option from the Export List, choose a directory to save to and file name and click ·OK.

Either way, FreeMind will try to open the new file if you have an application that can open it.

Print Preview

At this stage we've created a basic Mind Map, and we've also saved it and opened it. Once we've printed it out we've completed most of the fundamental tasks necessary to use the program. Before Printing, however, I generally suggest that you run a Print Preview. This is to make sure that you don't waste paper printing out something that you don't need to print out. In the File Menu click on Print Preview... .

At the top of the screen you'll see two arrows. The first is the back arrow, to go back a page, and the second is the forward arrow that goes to the next page.

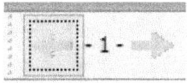

Make sure that you click the forward arrow to check on each page you will print out. You can zoom in or out and see how the page you are printing will appear in the window beneath the toolbar.

Page Setup

Often you will want to change the page setup either because you're printing to a different page format (i.e. A4, US Business letter format etc.), want to scale the diagram or change the layout from landscape to portrait or vice versa.

To control the page setup click on Page Setup... in the File Menu. You will see that a dialogue is opened that allows you to do Page Scaling first. Don't worry if you don't want to change the scale (i.e. make the diagram smaller) you can just press OK .

Scaling the Diagram

If you do want to change the scaling there are two ways that you can do it. My preferred option is to change the diagram automatically so that it fits into one page by clicking on the rectangle Fit to One Page .

You can also change the Zoom Factor for print by typing in a number into the print zoom factor box. The zoom factor starts as 1, with numbers higher than 1 zooming in to the picture, and numbers lower than 1 zooming out (i.e. getting smaller).

Print Zoom Factor (0.0 - 2.0): 1

If you are going to use the Print Zoom Factor I recommend using the Print Preview to see the effect of your changes. It can take a few experiments to see whether your setting is the right one for your diagram.

Once you're happy click OK to go to the main Page Setup dialogue.

Changing the Paper Size, Orientation or Margins

Click on the combo box under the Size dialogue to set the size of the paper in your printer. Most of these options are pretty self-explanatory. The paper sizes available depend on the printer drivers that you've installed although they are generally recognisable formats.

Click on the format that you want.

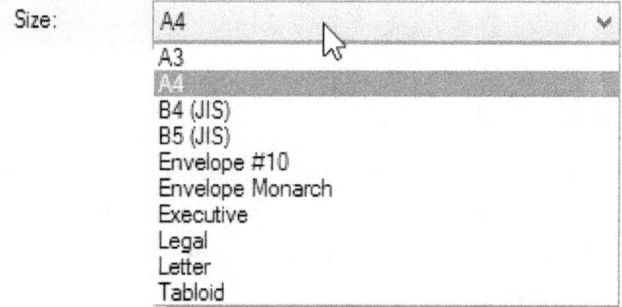

Once you've chosen your paper size you can edit your Orientation in the page setup.

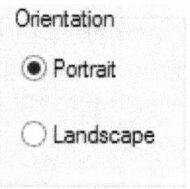

By default the orientation is Portrait, but you can click on the round circle next to Landscape in order to change the orientation from portrait to Landscape .

Margins are the blank spaces around the page which are used to prevent finger marks ending on the document or provide space for people to bind the work.

Margins (millimetres)

Left: 25.4   Right: 25.4

Top: 25.4   Bottom: 25.4

When you're happy with your Page Setup click OK . If you've made any substantial changes to the Page Setup you may want to run a print preview first.

Print

Once you are happy that you have set up the page correctly and the Print Preview seems correct click on 🖶 Print...   Ctrl+P   in the File menu to print the document. You will see a Print Dialogue. The first thing to do is to check that the Printer you are using is correct. You can see the current default printer in the box next to printer name

Name: Send To OneNote 2013   ⌄ .

If you are not sending the document to the right Printer click on the combobox next to name and select the correct Printer from the list.

Name: Send To OneNote 2013   ⌄
Fax
HP Deskjet 1050 J410 series
HP ePrint
Microsoft XPS Document Writer
Send To OneNote 2013

Once you've chosen the Printer check its status. It should read Status: Ready .

It's possible to control the range. By default you print out all pages.

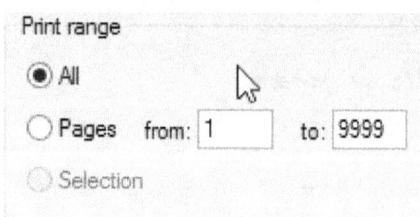

But you can print only specific pages by clicking on the circle next to  and entering a range in the boxes .

It is also possible to choose the number of copies by changing the textbox to a number higher than 1.

When you're happy click OK . Your document should start to print.

Next Chapter

In this chapter I've described how to create a basic Mind Map with FreeMind. I've shown you how to Open, Save, Create a new document, add nodes and move them as well as how to hide and show nodes and levels.

So we've covered most of the basic steps required to create a Mind Map.

The next chapter will build on these steps to help you to make a more attractive diagram.

Use FreeMind

2 DIAGRAM APPEARANCE

So far we've just created a very basic diagram.

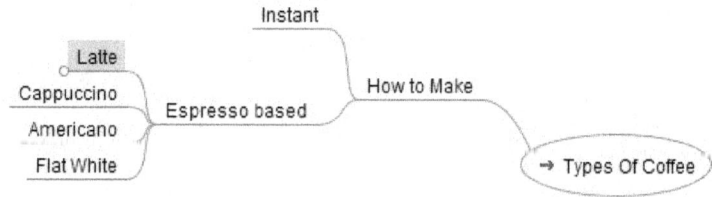

Now, in this chapter I'm going to show you how to edit the appearance of a diagram to make it substantially more interesting. Appearance changes aren't just used to make the diagram more appealing they can also be used to impart information as well.

Node Font and Size

Select the node whose font size or style you want to change.

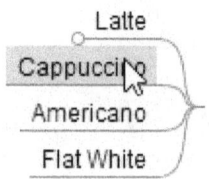

At the moment Cappuccino is in a plain ordinary default font. We want to make it stand out, so look in the toolbar and you'll see a font name and font size combo box.

Click on the Fontname box to see a long list of fonts. You can click on any of the fonts that you want, or scroll down using the scroll bar on the right until you find the right font. Sometimes you may need to experiment with font so remember that you can always use the undo 🔄 button if you aren't happy.

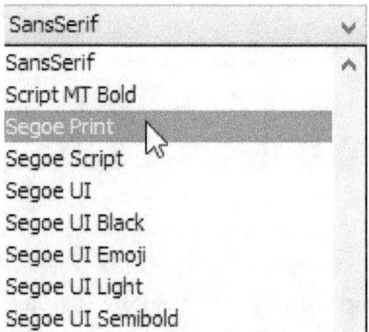

In this example I have chosen to use Segoe Print:

Each computer will have different fonts installed so you will have to choose a font that you like.

To change the size look for the combo box next to the font name. It'll have a number. 12 ∨ . Click on the box and you'll see a list of Font Sizes. Scroll down until you see the Font Size that you want, and then Click on it.

I often use the Size of the font to show the level of the node. For example, making the root node larger than level 1 nodes which are larger than level 2 nodes.

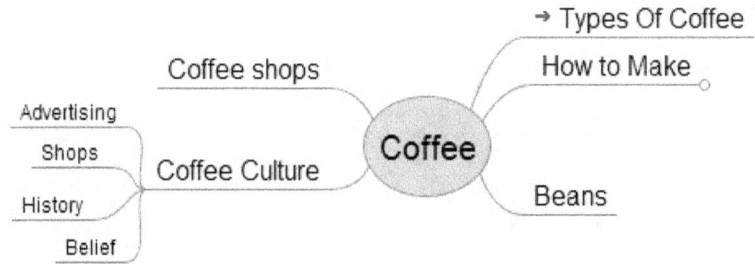

Other people use font size to visually display how important they consider a node is. So, Coffee Shops may be more important than Beans.

Emphasis

You can select a node that you want to give emphasis to, and then choose what type from the toolbar. For example italics *Advertising* by clicking on *i* , bold **Shops** by clicking on **b** .

More on Font Size

Above we changed the Font Size directly, i.e. using a number. But if you right click on a node, for example Shops in the Mind Map below:

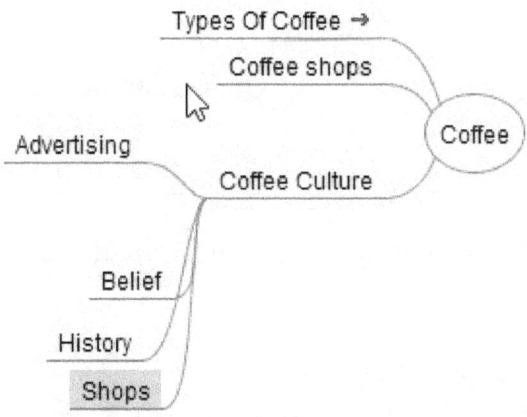

And hover your mouse over

Format ▸ you will see an

option to make the Font larger or smaller.

| Larger Font | Ctrl+Equals |
| Smaller Font | Ctrl+Minus |

This provides a way to increase the size of a node compared to nearby nodes without specifying an exact number.

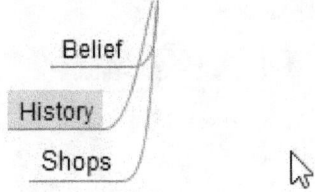

Using Cloud to group concepts.

One way of grouping related concepts together us using a cloud. You can group all child nodes together by selecting a branch node:

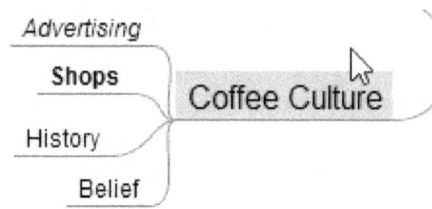

And then hitting the cloud button 🗨 in the toolbar to group them together:

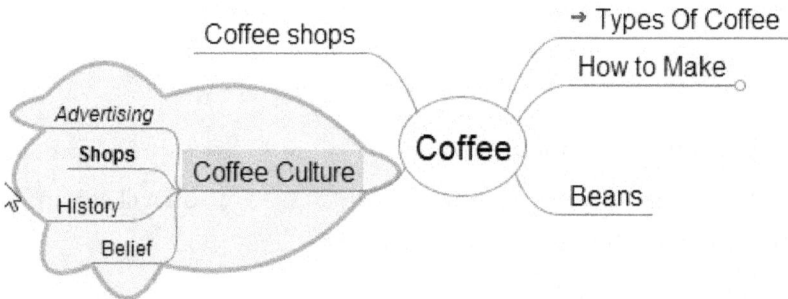

You can have sub clouds by clicking on the first node and then holding shift and clicking subsequent nodes until you've selected all the nodes that you need to select:

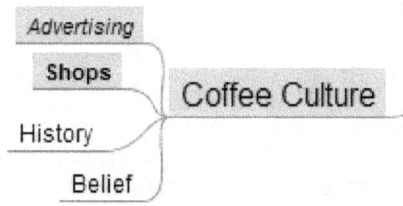

And then clicking on the cloud button 🗨 to group them together:

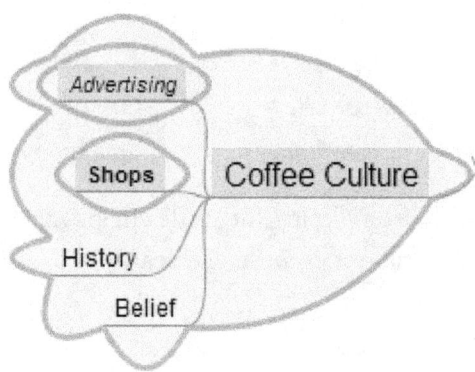

While it's a matter of taste more than anything I prefer not to use clouds very often, generally grouping together only very important concepts. Otherwise the diagram can become cluttered.

Indicating Order

Sometimes you may have a Mind Map where the order of tasks is very important. This is commonly the case where you're using the Mind Map as part of a Project Management or Task document. For example in the diagram below.

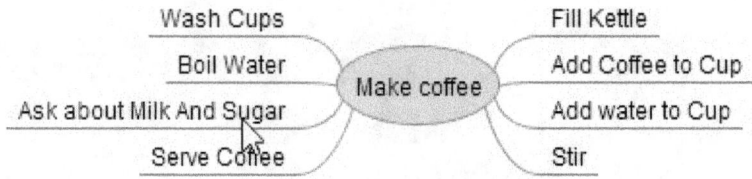

It really doesn't make sense to Fill Kettle after you Boil Water.

FreeMind allows you to show the order of steps that you are taking my moving the nodes as I showed you in the last chapter from the navigate menu:

Node Up	Ctrl+Up
Node Down	Ctrl+Down
Node Left	Ctrl+Left
Node Right	Ctrl+Right

On its own just ordering the nodes helps make sense of the diagram, but it's still not completely clear:

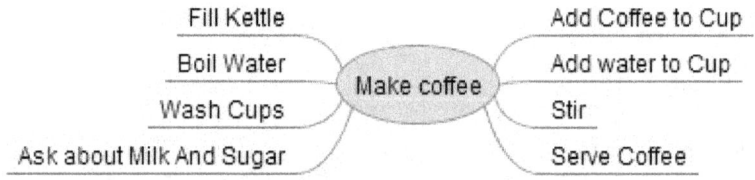

If you look at the left hand side of the screen you'll see the secondary toolbar. This toolbar contains a lot of graphics (known as Icons) that can be used to illustrate concepts. In particular, you'll see number bubbles from 0 to 9:

Select the first node that you want to number:

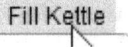

And click on the number you want to label the node from the Secondary Toolbar. I'm going to number it .

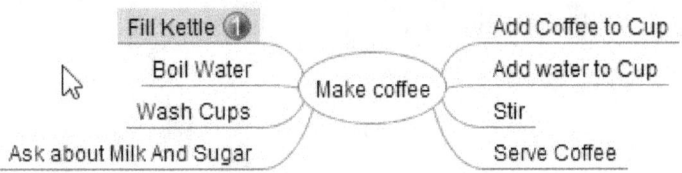

You can repeat the process until you've numbered all the nodes in order. Note that you can label several different nodes with the same number, for example if they are both part of the same process.

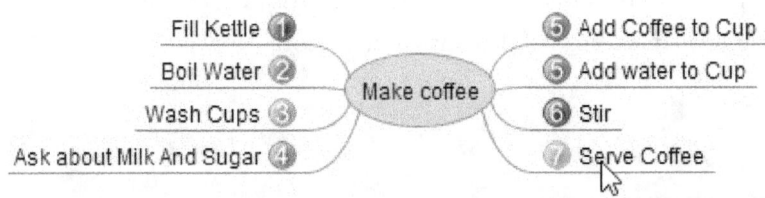

Obviously, these numbers can be used for other purposes such as giving nodes a priority, or even an importance score from 0 to 9.

That's the case with many of these icons. Although there may be an "official" interpretation you shouldn't worry if you use the interpretation that is most useful to your diagram.

Showing Status of Project

Sometimes you may want to show the status of a project. You may want to use traffic lights to show whether a task is running smoothly , might be of concern or is in trouble .

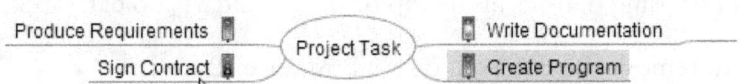

Other Useful Icons

There are a number of other Icons that you can use, including icons that show you the type of node (whether it's an idea, a question, important, very important, something that is for information, and something that will stop the project or a problem)

Another important icon is the tick or cross which can be used to say whether a task has been completed or not.

Clearly, there are dozens of other icons that will be useful in one circumstance or another. The best way is to look through the icons and choose ones that cover the concept that you want to illustrate.

Removing an Icon.

Say that you're working on a project and – miracle of miracles – the project status changes so a problem task is completed. You'll want to change the status:

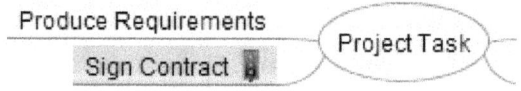

To do this you need to remove the icon from that node. You can do so using buttons at the top of the secondary toolbar. Click on ✕ to remove the last icon, or 🗑 to remove all icons.

In addition you can right click on a node and hover your mouse over ⎸Icons⎸ to see a list of icons and their official purposes.

If you don't see the icon that you want, hover your mouse over More or More… 1 to see even more icons.

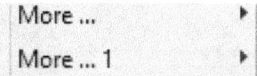

Showing Icon Hierarchically

By default FreeMind will show icons on individual nodes. If you give a child node an icon it won't show up as an icon on the parent node.

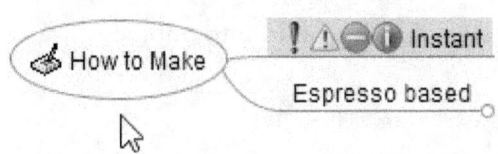

It's possible to make it so that any icon in a child node is also displayed in the parent node by clicking on Show Icons Hierarchically in the Format menu.

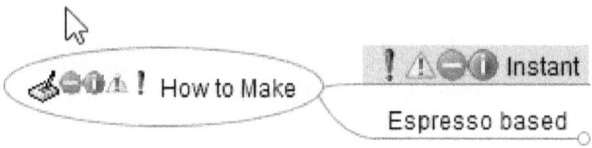

You can toggle it off again by clicking on

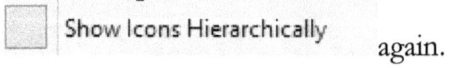

again.

Node Style – Fork or Bubble

We've already seen the default child node style, the Fork. But it's also possible to make a node into a bubble like the Root Node without making it the Root Node. This highlights something so you're almost making a sub-mind map. For example, if you select Sign Contract below:

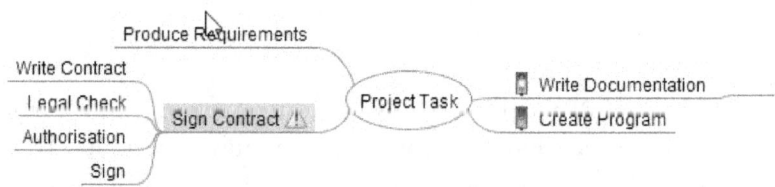

And then click on

Bubble

you will see that the node and all the child nodes turn into bubbles.

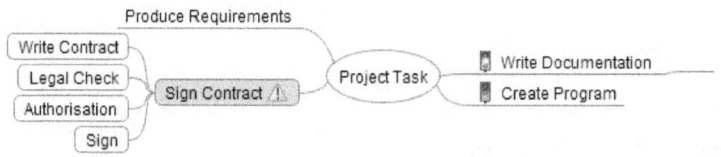

Sometimes, you may want to remove the bubbles from the child nodes. You can do this by selecting the first child node, then holding shift before clicking on each child node in turn. When you've selected all the child nodes let go:

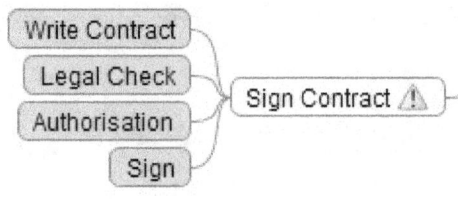

And then clicking on   Fork
in the Format menu.

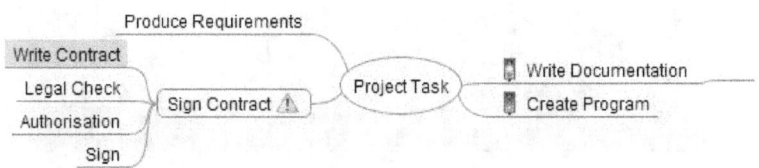

Node Colour (Text)

Sometimes you may want to highlight a node by changing its colour. This might be the case if concepts have a particular colour associated with them – for example, political parties in the United Kingdom:

Labour is associated with the colour Red, so if we right click on it, hover the mouse
over   Format   ▸ and then
choose   Node Color...   Alt+Shift+F from the
context sensitive menu we'll see a Colour dialogue. By default we are choosing a colour using swatches, but you can also choose a colour using different colour pickers, such as a Hue Saturation Value (HSV)

colour picker etc.

You can see a tab with the different colour pickers at the top of the screen.

For the moment, just choose a colour from the block of colours (remember, Labour is Red)

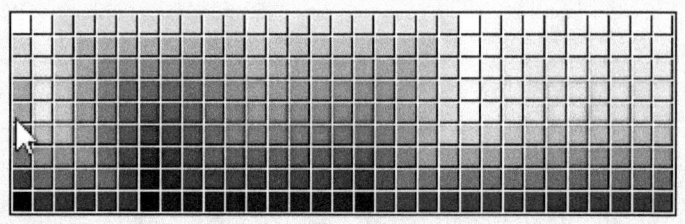

You'll see a preview of the choice that you have made:

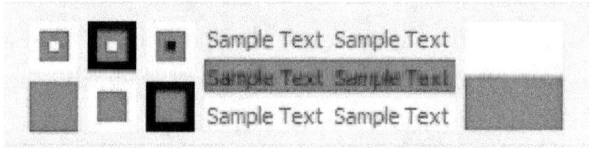

If you are happy with it click on OK .

Using Other Colour Pickers

While Swatches will often give you a good enough choice to go on with, you'll sometimes find that they don't give you precisely the right value. There are several other colour pickers that you can use once you've opened the Node Colour Dialogue using the steps above.

In the dialogue, click on one of the other Picker tabs. In this example I'm going to choose HSV.

This dialogue looks complex at first:

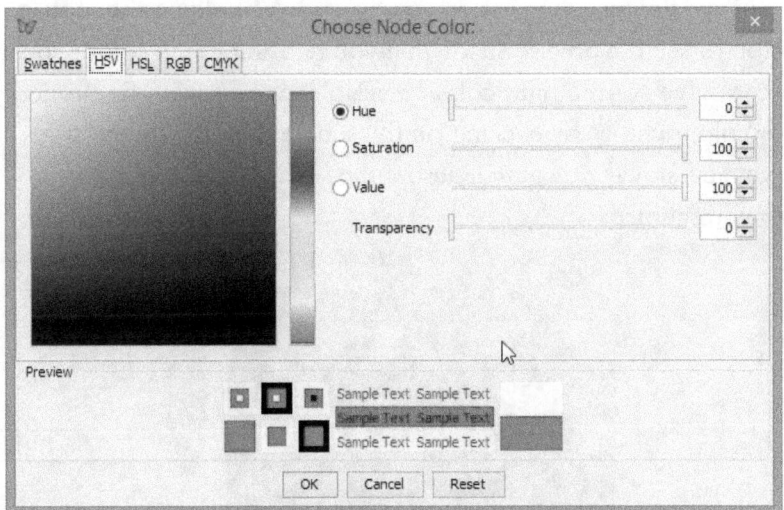

The first step when using it is to use the colour bar to select the basic hue you want. Move your mouse over it, and click in approximately the right place for the basic colour that you want to insert.

Move the mouse up or down while you're holding the mouse button to see the precise shade that you're using in the colour square. Once you've got the right colour available in the square fine-tuned your colour choice by clicking on the square, holding the mouse down, and slowly dragging it across the square until you're happy with your choice.

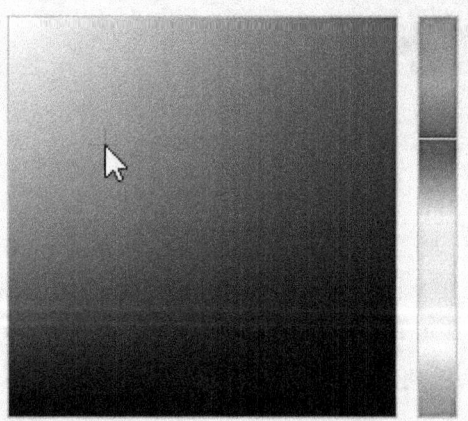

You can fine tune your choice further using the slide bars on the right hand side, although I find that this isn't as useful as using the colour square. When you move the slide bar you will see that the colour point (i.e. the square) will move. For example, if you change saturation the point will move to the left or right becoming greyer or more intense.

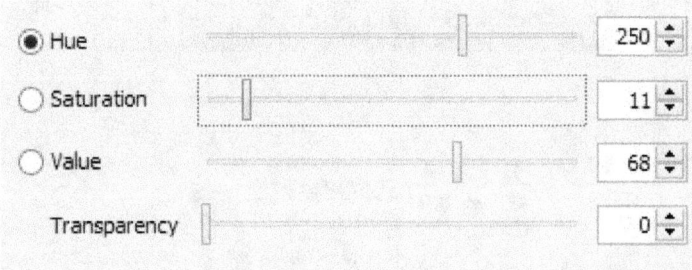

It is useful to check the Preview when you think you're happy with your choice, and then click on OK .

There is another button that is interesting, the Reset button, which returns the colour choice to the one that you had before you changed the colour. The dialogue will remain open, whereas Cancel will close the dialogue.

Node Background Colour

Just as you can change the text colour of a node you can also change the background colour of the node. Right click on the node you want to change and hover your mouse over Format ▸ and then select Node Background Color... which will show you a colour selection dialogue like the one that you used in the last section.

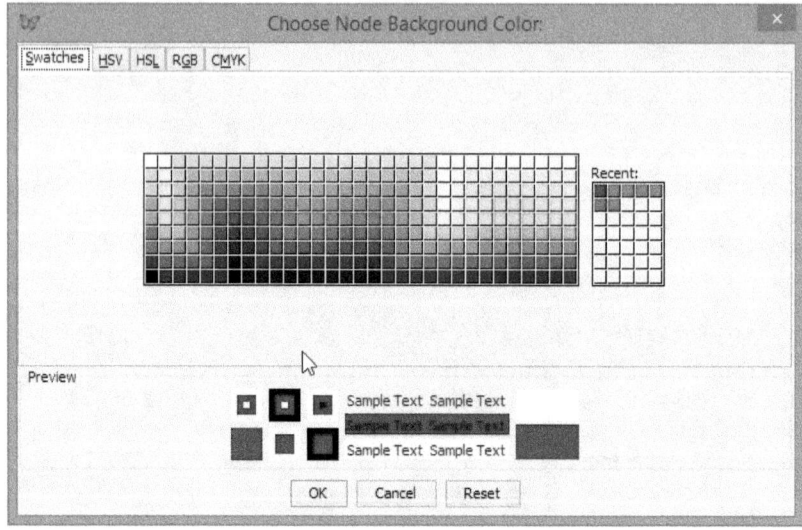

Choose the colour that you want to use, either from the swatch colour picker or one of the other colour pickers from the Picker tab 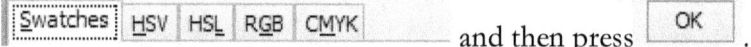 and then press OK .
Sometimes, as in the below example, changing the background colour may make the text hard to read:

In which case I recommend also changing the Node Colour (see the last section) so that you have light text on a dark background or vice versa:

Removing the Node Background Colour

Sometimes when you've added a background colour you may want to remove it. For example, given the example below, you may want to remove the blue from the conservative node:

While you could do this using the Node Background Colour options an easier method is to right click on the node, hover your mouse over Format ▸ and then use Remove Node Background Color to remove the colour.

One thing to watch out for is that if you have changed the text colour to white as in the previous example, removing the background colour will result in you not being able to read the node!

But simply changing the Node colour back to black will make it easily readable.

Copy and Paste Node Format

When you've worked hard to make a node appear the way you want it to it can be useful to use the format on a similar node. One way to do this is to make a new Physical Style (and I tell you how to do this latter in the book) but sometimes you may only want to use the same formatting once or twice.

Select the nodes whose formatting you want to copy:

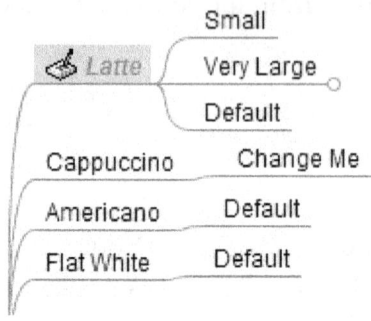

Then <image ✎> Copy Format   Alt+C   in the Edit menu. Then select the Node you want to paste the format to and click on Paste Format   Alt+V   in the Edit Menu.

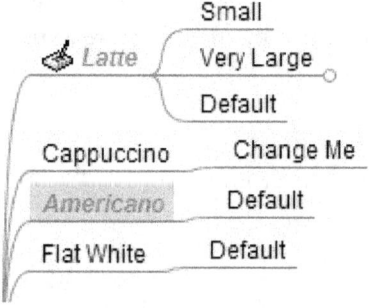

Remember, it is sometimes better to use a Physical Style rather than just paste formats.

Edge Appearance

We've come across edges throughout this book. An edge is a line between a node and a child node! Just as we can change the appearance of a node we can also change the style and appearance of an edge.

Edge Width

To change the appearance of a single edge, the first step is to right click on the child node. So, if you want to change the appearance of the edge from Labour to Political Party click on Labour rather than Political Party.

If on the other hand you want to change all edges going from a node, click on the parent node.

The reason for this is that if you select a node, and change the edge properties, all edges from that node will change to include the properties that you've chosen.

So, in our example we've chosen to right click on Labour. Now we hover our mouse over

Format ▸ and then over

Edge Widths ▸ to show a list of edge widths that we can change to. The default is the edge will be the same as the parent.

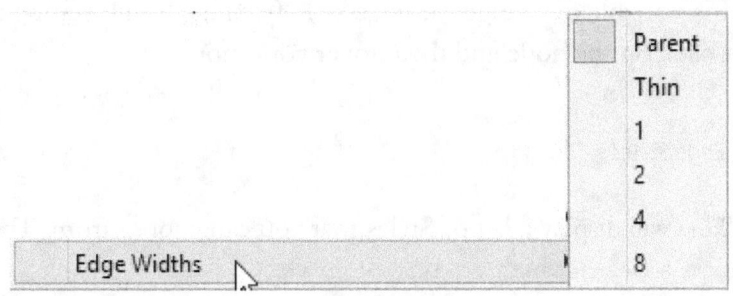

We can choose a range of non-default options from very thin to the thickest. In this case, I've chosen 8:

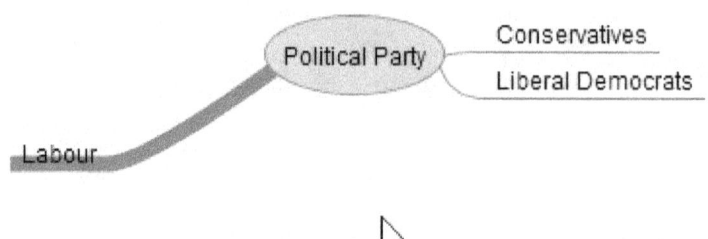

If you repeat the process with the Root Node Political Party, choosing a width of 2 you'll see that all edges changed except Labour which isn't set to default to the Parent width.

We could change this by selecting Parent as our Line Width instead of Thin or a number.

Edge Style

It's possible to change the edge style from its default setting too. Right click on the node and then hover your mouse over Format and

Edge Styles .

This will display a list of Styles that you can choose from. The default is a Bezier which is a type of curve.

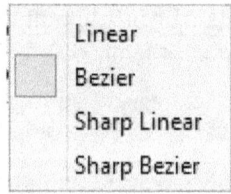

You can see what I mean more easily if I change labour to Linear. It becomes just a straight line, compared to Liberal Democrats which has a curve associated with it.

Try out Sharp Linear and Sharp Bezier to see what they do too.

Edge Colour

It's not just Node colour that you can change. You can also change the Edge Colour as well. Remember, by default if you change the Edge colour of a parent node all edges leaving it will change to match the style. If you change the Edge Colour of a child node it will change the edge from it to the Parent as well as any Child Nodes the Node has.

Right click on the Node that you want to change, then hover your mouse over Format ▶

and click on Edge Color... Alt+Shift+E to display the edge colour dialogue.

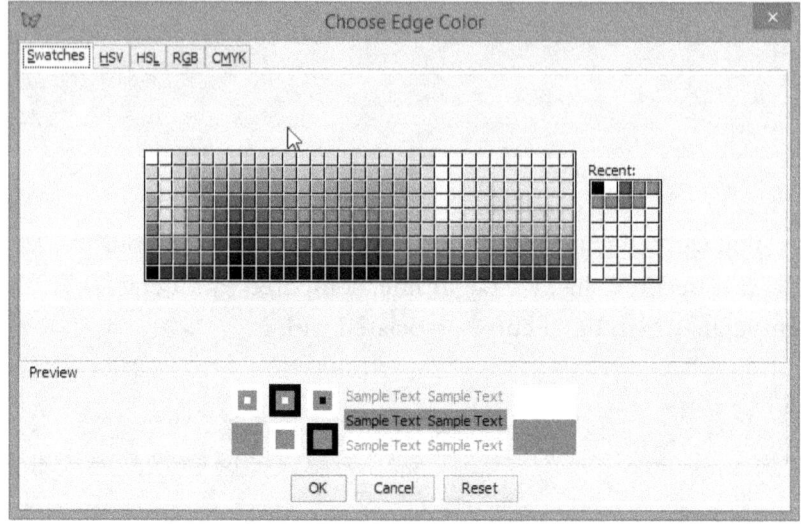

You can use this dialogue in the same way that you used the Node Background Colour Dialogue to select the best colour for the edge. For example, Red.

Adding an Image Link

Say you have concepts that are linked. For example, you may be creating a Development mind map, and think that the Evaluation stage links into creating new requirements:

So far there's been no way that you can link two nodes together. But if you select all the nodes that you want to link together:

(Remember, if you hold ctrl before clicking you will select multiple nodes).

And then in the Insert menu click
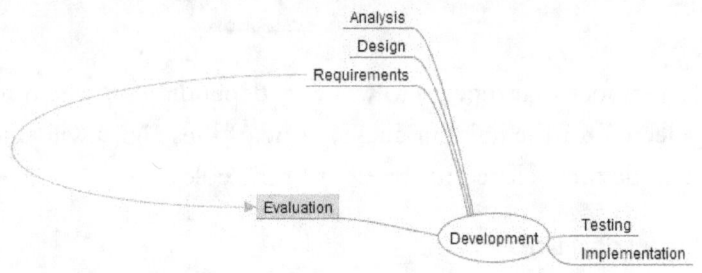 you will see a new Graphical link appear:

I find that you sometimes have to move the nodes a little bit to stop them crossing over too much and looking bad.

Now, there's something wrong with the above diagram... the arrow is in the wrong direction. Right click on the link and you'll see a number of line styles.

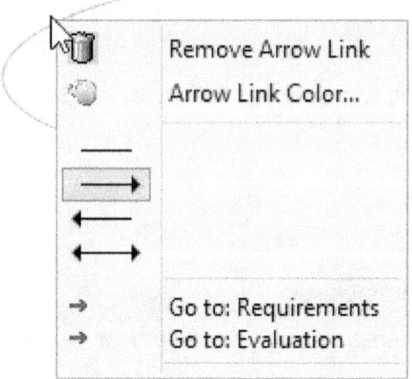

You can also delete it by clicking 🗑   Remove Arrow Link or change the line colour by clicking 🎨   Arrow Link Color... which brings up a colour picking dialog.

Below the different arrow types you'll see two links.

→   Go to: Requirements
→   Go to: Evaluation

The nodes that they go to will vary depending on which nodes you selected for the link but clicking one of these links will take you to the node that is listed to the right of the colon.

Adding a Local Link

A graphical link doesn't automatically take you to the node that it is pointing to. But it's often useful to provide a link that will do just that. Local Links are a facility that FreeMind provides that allows the user to double click on a node and go instantly to the linked node.

The order that you select the nodes in is important. The first node that you select is the origin node (the node the user will click on) and the second node is the destination node. Click on the Origin node to select it:

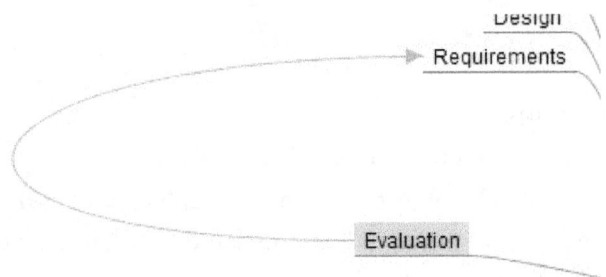

Then press and hold ctrl, click on Requirements and let go of ctrl to select the two nodes:

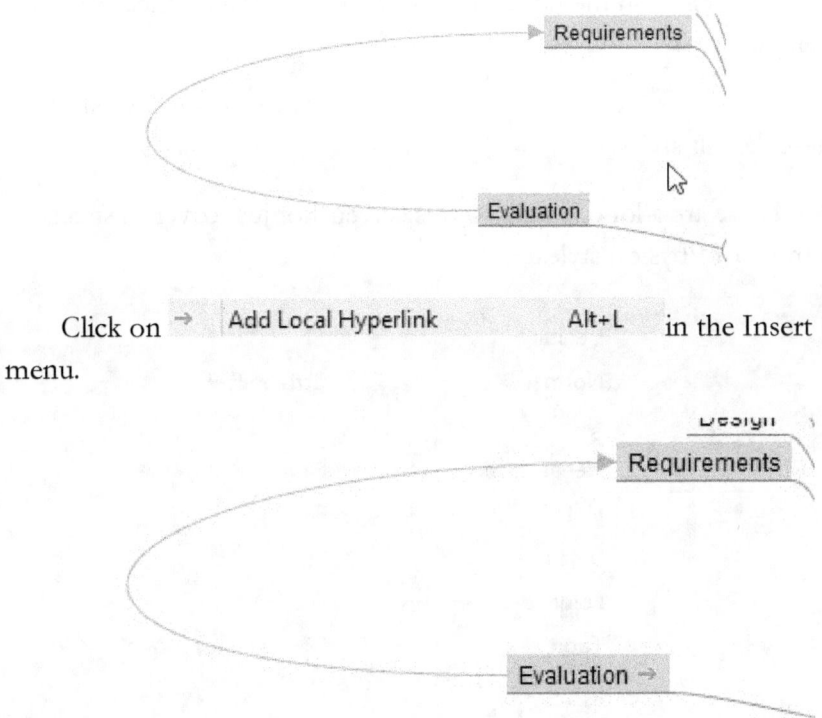

Click on → Add Local Hyperlink Alt+L in the Insert menu.

Note the green arrow. This means that you're using a local link. Double clicking on the link will take you to the destination node but FreeMind may prompt you to save the file first before going to the node if you've edited the mind map without saving it.

Physical Styles

FreeMind has already created styles for individual nodes that reflect concepts like objects of code, topic, Needs action, OK etc. It calls these Physical Styles. While you can do the same kind of things yourself through manually changing the styles it can be helpful to use the Physical Styles so that your diagrams are consistent throughout your organisation.

Right click on the node that you want to give a Physical Style to, then hover your mouse over

Physical Style   ▶ to show a list of

these default styles.

There are a lot of them, so this screenshot just covers a small number of Physical styles.

Default	F1
Normal	Ctrl+Shift+N
OK	F3
Needs action	F4
Hot	F5
Detail	F6
Folder	F7
Topic	F8
Larger Topic	F9
Waiting Topic	Ctrl+F1
Object / Keyword	Ctrl+F2

For example, if I choose   Hot   F5
we can see the new Physical style.

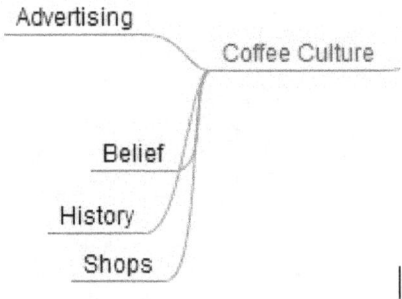

Managing Physical Styles

While FreeMind has already got a set of Standard Styles that the developers thought most people would find useful it has also got a way of altering them or adding new styles to your Diagram. This allows you to give your Mind Maps a unique look and feel as well as attach styles to issues or concepts that are important to your project.

Modifying an Existing Pattern

Right click on a node, and hover your mouse over

Physical Style ▸ then click

on Manage Patterns...   F11 . This will show the Manage Patterns dialogue which can be quite intimidating at first.

On the left hand side of the screen are a range of Physical Styles – for example Hot. If you click on a style you can change the appearance of that style.

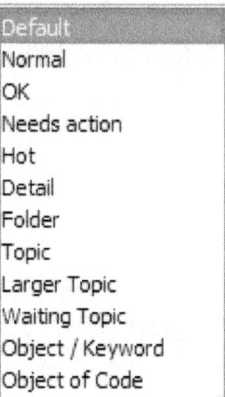

For example, if I select Hot I'll see the values for that style. On the Right hand side we see quite a range of different properties. For example, as we saw earlier the Node Color is changed to Red for the Hot Physical Style.

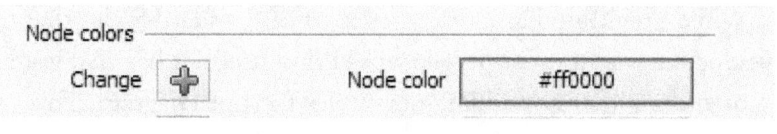

A style that has a plus in the Change box Change ✚ will change that property in any nodes that have the same physical style. If you leave it empty Change ☐ then the property won't have any effect on the nodes. An example font size. By default, the Hot Physical Style doesn't change it.

Change ☐ Node's font size 2 ⌄

A more complicated one is the Change ⚊ . This will set that property to the default value.

Let's say we want to change the Node Background Colour for hot Yellow. We scroll down in the list of properties until we can see it.

Then we click on the change box 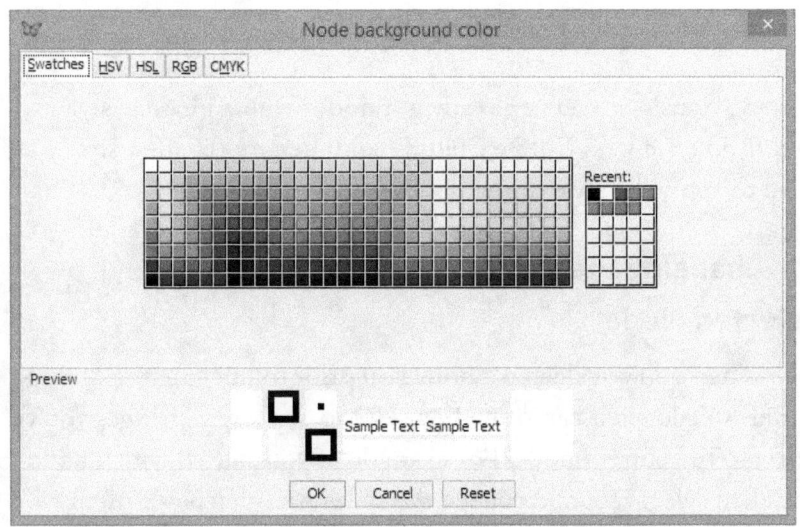to make it a +. This means we're going to add the background colour to any node with a Hot Physical Style.

Finally, we click the property box

to bring up a colour dialogue, and choose yellow.

Note that the value changes in the property box. (The number is actually a special code that programmers use to refer to a particular colour).

Change ✛ Node background color #ffff00

When you've finished editing the Physical Styles for the document, click on Save and Return.

One thing you'll see is that the appearance of the box hasn't changed. Any changes you make to Physical Styles are not retrospective, but if you were to select a node such as Advertising and apply the physical style Hot to it you'd see that we really have made a difference to the appearance of the physical style:

Obviously, if you've already got nodes with a physical style (we've got one with Coffee Culture) and then modify that style you'll have to apply the style to the node again.

Changing the Physical Style of the Currently Selected Node

When you've selected a node you prior to opening the Manage Patterns dialogue it can often be useful to apply any changes you've made to the current node. For example, if you started with a node and then select Hot and change the styles parameters it's often because you want to make the node you selected have the new parameters.

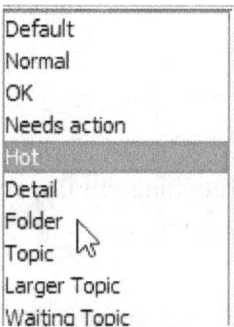

Above, we've selected Hot in the styles list. If we want to apply the changes we've made to the currently selected node in the diagram all we need to do is use the Actions menu. Click on Apply in the Actions menu and the selected style will be applied to the currently selected node.

Child Patterns

Sometimes, you may want to control the style of a child node when you apply the style to its parent. For example, if you have a hot style you may want to change any child nodes to Needs Action. To do this you need to look at the General options, and change the Child Pattern.

First, click on the Change box until it shows 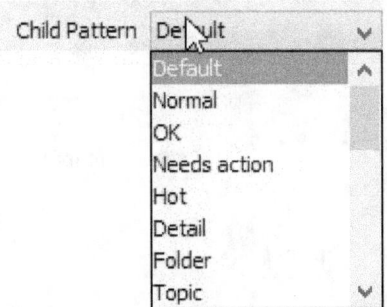.
Then select the style that you want my clicking on the combo box next to Child Pattern to produce a list of available patterns:

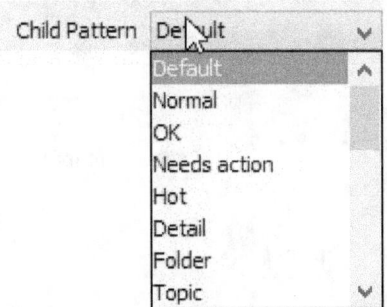

Click on the pattern that you want to use:

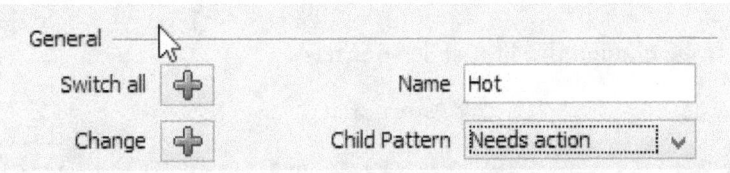

Click on  and then apply the Hot style to a parent node:

Note that if you use

it will change child nodes to the default style. This won't necessarily change child nodes of Child nodes, however, so it's important to be aware that the Child Pattern Property only works for one level at a time. Take the following diagram:

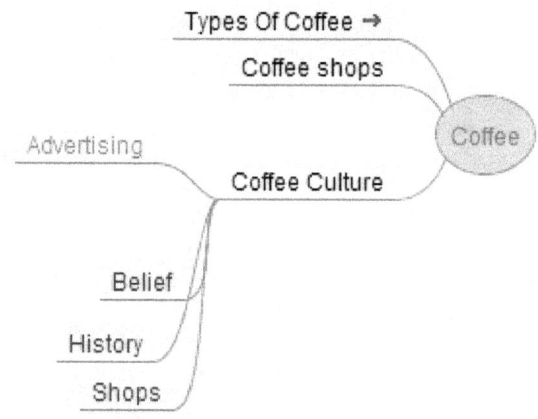

If we change the Hot style so it has

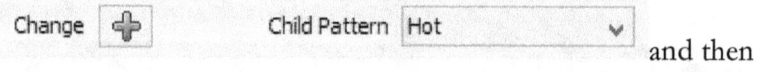

and then apply the Hot style to the root node we'll see that not only the Child nodes but *their* child nodes change to hot.

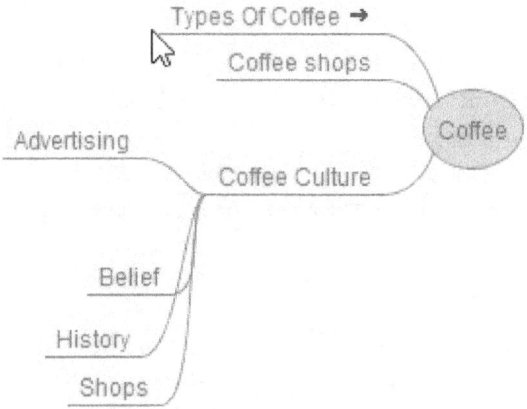

This is because when the root node has the hot style applied to it, the root will apply hot to its' child nodes, and so on.

Adding a New Style based on the currently selected node

It is a bit tricky to change the parameters using the above method. Sometimes you just want to change parameters such as if the node is bold or italic, font size, colour and so on using the methods I've already shown you in the chapter.

But when we have a node looking the way we want it, we realise that it would be useful to be able to apply all the same parameters to additional nodes: or, in other words, create a new style based on a particular node.

Say, we've created the following

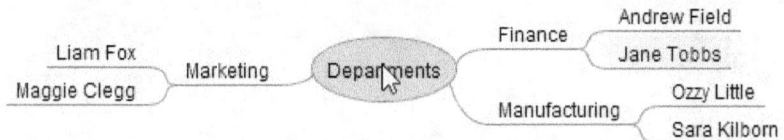

Jane Tobbs is the department head. If we want to create a style based on the formatting for Jane Tobbs, we can select her node and

| Manage Patterns... | F11 |

from the Physical Style option in the context sensitive menu as normal. This will display the Manage Patterns dialogue.

Click on Create Pattern From Selected Nodes in the Action menu.

Change the Name | New Pattern | field to contain the name that you want the style to have. For example, Name | Department Head| .

You can change the properties in the same way that I've shown you previously, for example changing the font size or edge colour.

Then, when you're happy click on Save and Return . When you go to change the Physical Style of a node you'll see that the list includes your new style.

MindMapDefault
Department Head   Physical Style

Here is the completed Department MindMap using the new style for Department Heads:

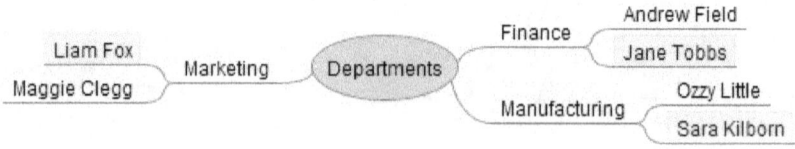

Adding a New Style using parameters

To be honest I don't often use this option but it's possible to create a new style from scratch in the Manage Patterns dialogue by clicking on   Add new Pattern   .Make sure that you give the new pattern a name   Name New Pattern   . After that you'll have to enable the   Change   boxes and supply parameters from scratch.

Honestly, I find that it's better to create a style from a node rather than try to do it manually, but this is an option if you want it.

Reverting a node to the Default Style

Select the node and then Press F1 (function key 1, right at the top of the keyboard often next to the escape. You may need to hold the fn key on some keyboards) to revert a node to the default style. You can also right click on a node, hover your mouse over   Physical Style   ▸ and select Default   F1   .

Reverting entire diagram to the default style.

To revert the entire diagram to the default style first select the root node, and click on ✚ Unfold All   Alt+End   in the navigate menu. Then select all the nodes by clicking on Select All Visible   Ctrl+A   in the Edit menu, and finally press F1 or select Default from the Physical Style list in the contest sensitive menu for root.

You'll have to click off (i.e. click on the white space around the diagram) to see the effect of this.

Sorting Child Nodes

As you add Child Nodes to a Mind Map you'll often find that ideas come to you in a slightly disorganised way. Often it can help you to add ideas without worrying too much about alphabetical order.

If you want nodes sorted into alphabetical order (and sometimes you might not. Instead you might want to order them according to some other criterion) you can do it automatically by selecting the Parent Node, and then   Sort Children   in the Tools Menu.

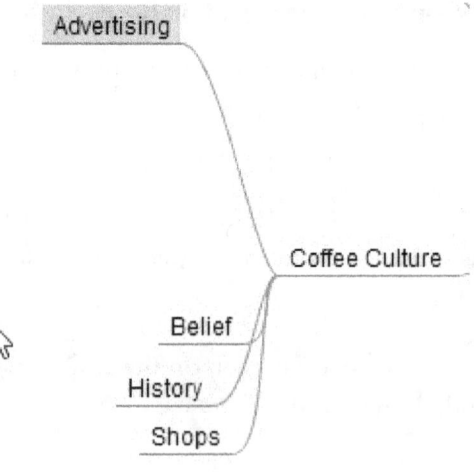

You'll often find that you'll need to manually adjust the exact position of the nodes after a sort so I generally suggest waiting to move nodes until you've finished making the Mind Map in case you need to run a sort.

Next Chapter

In this chapter I've tried to explain some of the ways that you will improve the appearance of the Mind Map that you have created.

The next chapter will cover more advanced features that you use to Edit and improve the look of the document.

3 EDITING THE DOCUMENT

So far we've created a mind map and made it look good. This chapter is all about editing the document, adding useful information to each node, adding images and generally improving the usability of the Mind Map.

Returning an Node to the Original Position

Sometimes when moving nodes around the screen you may decide you've made a mistake. It can be hard for you to return the node to the original (default) position because you can't see it.

First, select the node. Then click on Reset Position in the Format menu. You'll see that it reverts the node to the position it was when it was added to the diagram.

Selecting Visible

To select all the nodes that are visible in a branch click on Select Visible Branch Ctrl+Shift+A in the Edit menu. For example, if we select Latte and then run a Select Visible Branch all the child nodes of Latte are selected.

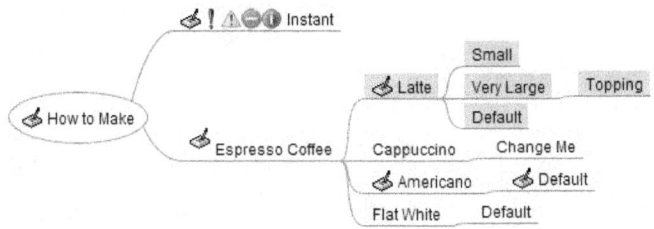

To select all visible nodes click

on Select All Visible   Ctrl+A in the Edit menu.

Edit Node

So far we've briefly talked about the Note Window but not talked about the formatting that you can use within it. Remember that the note window is below the Mind Map view:

And if it's not visible you can turn it on by clicking

Note Window   Ctrl+Shift+Less in the View menu.

We use the Note window to add more information about a topic area, typing in text that is relevant to the particular node.

Undo and Redo

When you make a mistake click ↰ to perform a single step undo, and if you change your mind click ↱ to redo the step.

Selecting text

Select text by going to the end of the text you want to highlight with your mouse

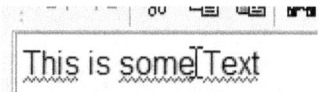

Then clicking and holding the mouse button and moving the mouse to the beginning of the text that you want to select. Let go of the mouse button.

Cut Copy and Paste

Select the text that you want to copy or cut.

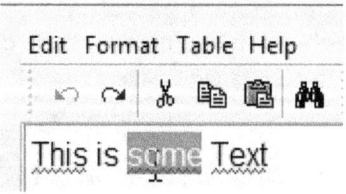

Copy records the selected text in memory without changing it. Press 🗐 to copy the text. Cut makes a copy of the text in memory and then deletes it. Press ✂ to cut:

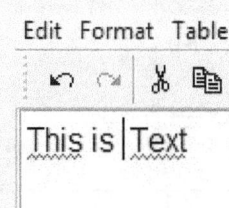

Either way, go to the location you want to paste to and then press ![] . For example if I go to the end of the sentence and paste the text I'll see:

You can cut text from other applications and then paste into FreeMind. This can speed up the process of making documents.

Change Font

The first step if you want to change the font is to select the text that you want to change.

> Change the font of a word is easy

At the top of the Note Window next to the Find icon (![]) is a font combo box which if you click gives you a list of fonts. Select the font from the list that you want.

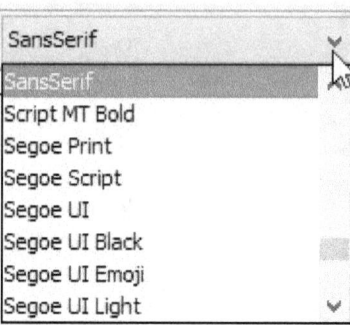

You will see the font of your selection change:

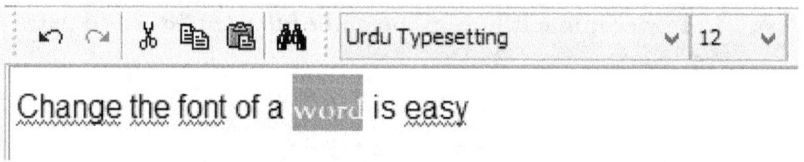

To the right of it is a font size combo box which when you click it gives you a number of font sizes you can choose from. Click on one of the font sizes to change the size of the selected text.

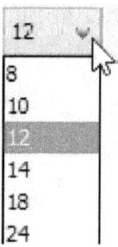

Select some text and click **b** to make it bold, *i* to make it italic, <u>U</u> to make it underlined, or T to bring up a colour selection dialog.

Bold, *italics*, <u>underline</u>, colour

If you change your mind and want to remove the formatting select text and then click ⊘ .

Alignment controls the placement of the entire paragraph

(although you can change the alignment of multiple paragraphs by selecting more than one paragraph at a time). Click ≣ to make the paragraph left aligned, ≣ to make it centre aligned, and ≣ to make it right aligned.

Bullet lists

It's often useful to make a bullet list.

Start on a blank line, and then press ≔ and then type until you finish your point then press enter. Add another point, press enter, and repeat the process until you've finished making the entire list. Then press enter a second time. The bullet list will automatically toggle off.

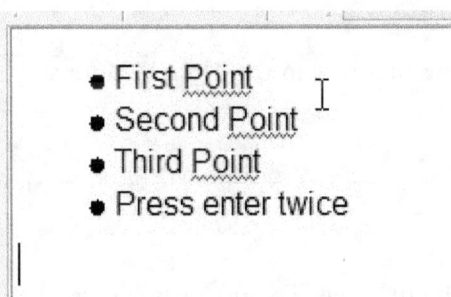

Press ≔ to make a numbered list using the same process that you just used for a bullet list.

1. First Point
2. Second Point
3. Third Point
4. Press enter twice

Tables

Sometimes when making a large note you'll want to include a table of information. To create a table click on [Table...] in the Table menu. Then select the number of columns that you want the table to include.

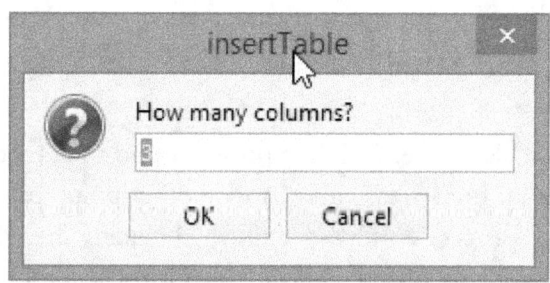

And press [OK].

You'll see the first row in the Note Window.

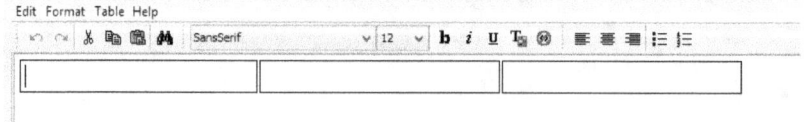

Click into the first cell. To add a row below the currently selected row click on Append row in the Table Menu. To insert above the currently selected row click on Insert row .

Inserted Row		
Selected row		
Appended Row		

Click into a cell to edit it. If you want to delete a row click on any cell in the row and then ⊟⁺ Delete row in the Table menu.

For example, after click into the middle cell and editing it I decide to delete it.

Inserted Row		
Selected row	Editing this row|	
Appended Row		

Clicking ⊟⁺ Delete row produces:

Inserted Row		
Appended Row			

Ψ Delete column works in the same way, although you can see that the next column increases in size when you delete the Colum.

Inserted Row		
Appended Row		

You'll find that ⼟ Insert column adds a column to the left, and Append col adds a column to the right.

Inserted Column	Selected Column	Appended Column
	Selected Column	

You can edit the appearance of the text in the same way that you edit any other text in the Note Window.

Find and Replace in the Node Window

Click on ⚲ to find text within the Note Window. This will bring up a dialogue where you can enter the text to

find **Text to find:** [Selected ⌄] . When you click on

[Find next...] it will find the next example of the text in the Note Window.

Inserted Column	Selected Column	Appended Column
	Selected Column	

You can keep on clicking [Find next...] to go to the next instance until there are no more instances to find at which point it will inform you that it's reached the end of the note.

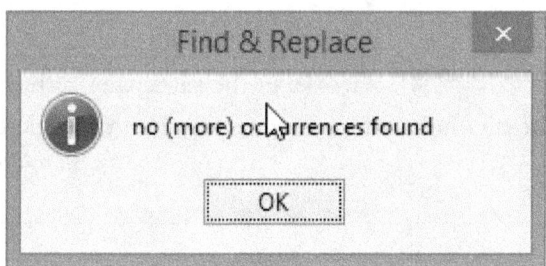

By default it will search down from the top of the screen, but you can change this in the Options by clicking the square by ☑ Search from start . It searches down unless you click the circle by ○ Search up .

You can also click on the squares by the options to Match the case (otherwise by default FreeMind will consider AAA the same as aAa and AAa etc.), to match whole words (so cat wouldn't match with catapult) and an approximate search.

☐ Match case   ☐ Match Approximately
☐ Whole words only

Finally, if you want to replace text that you've found with other

text type into the box   Replace with: [   ] and

click   [Replace…] . If you don't want to replace a particular

instance of text you can click [Find next…] to find the next item
that matches the search.

Click [Close] to close the Find window.

Find

Just as search and replace in the Note Window is very useful it's
also quite useful to be able to search and replace in the main Mind
Map.

To Find click on 🔍 Find…   Ctrl+F   in
the Edit menu which will bring up a find dialogue. Enter the text that
you want to search into the dialogue.

By default the main Find will search through both the Node text
and any Notes that you've made ☑ Also Search in Notes to find the text.
If you want click the ☑ to turn this feature off so that it only
searches through the Node text.

Either way, when you click 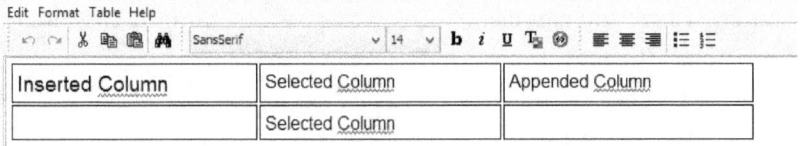 Ok it will search through the Nodes in order until it finds the text, either in the Node or in the Node Notes if appropriate. It will select the first node that if finds with the text that you're interested in.

For example, the Instant Node has the text "Selected" in its' Note text:

Edit Format Table Help		
Inserted Column	Selected Column	Appended Column
	Selected Column	

And so when we search with the following settings:

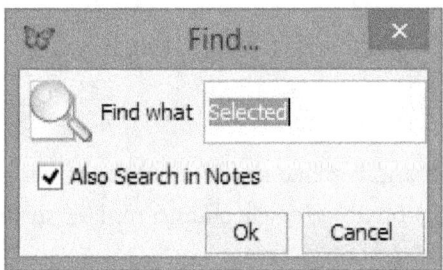

FreeMind selects the node automatically even though the text is in the Note.

It's all very well to search for the first instance but what happens if we want to search through the document? You can search for the next instance by using Find Next   Ctrl+G in the Edit Menu. It will keep on searching through the document until there are no more items to be found:

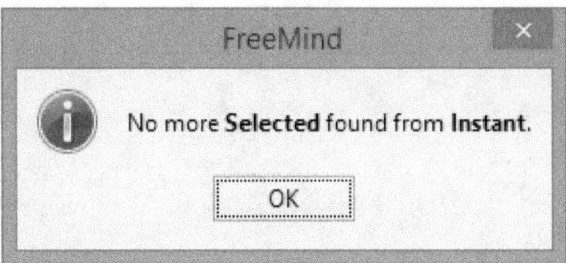

Each time you use

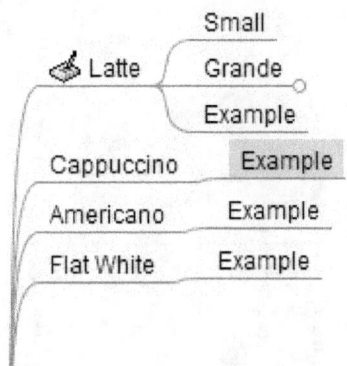 Find...   Ctrl+F   from the Edit menu you

start the search at the first item again.

Replace

While it's good to be able to search for things there are many times when you also want to replace a piece of text with another piece of text. To do this, click

on   Find and Replace...   Ctrl+Shift+F in the Edit menu.

Say we have the following Mind Map:

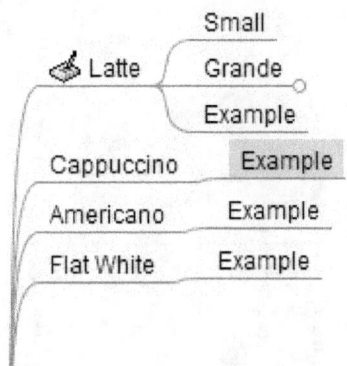

First, let's run the Find and Replace dialogue by clicking

Find and Replace...   Ctrl+Shift+F in the Edit menu. This

dialogue looks a little bit more complicated than any Find and Replace dialogue that we've seen so far but we start using it by typing in the Find box:

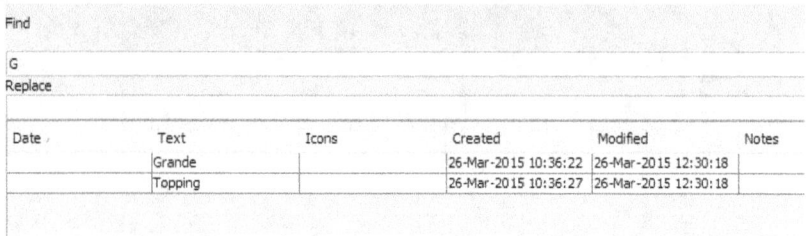

As you can see FreeMind starts to search from the very first letter you type. Keep an eye on the search results. We keep on typing, and then we see that:

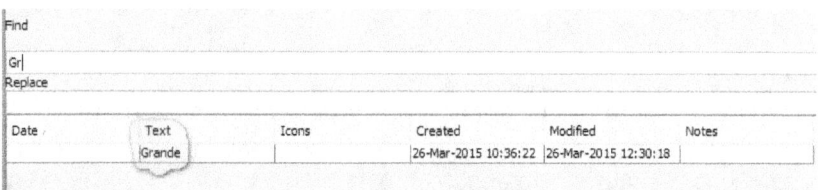

Just typing in Gr found all the examples of Grande. It's still important to type the rest of the text that you want to replace since FreeMind will only replace the text that it sees in the Find Box.

Now, type in the text that we want to replace the selection with into the Replace box:

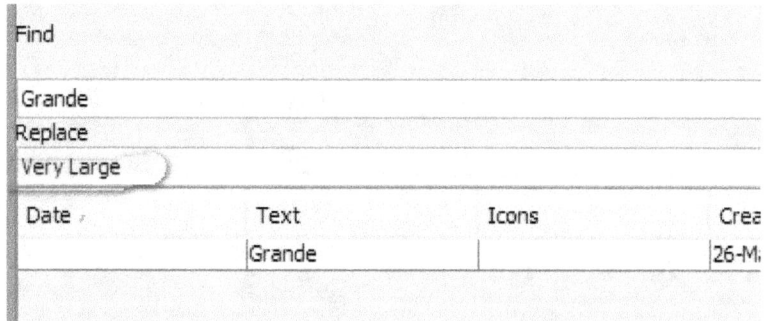

(One thing to note is if we leave the Replace box blank it means we're going to delete the Find text and not replace it with anything).

Because we've only found one result we just click Replace All   Ctrl+Shift+R in the Action Menu:

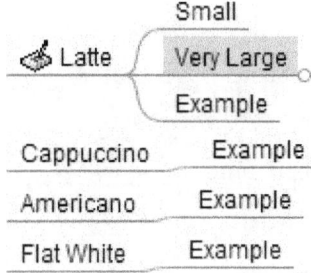

FreeMind will only replace the text that it finds from the Find Box. For example if you were searching for "Extra Grande" , then Finding "Extra" and replacing it with "Massive" would make it read "Massive Grande".

What happens if you have more than one result?

Find		
Example		
Replace		
Default		
Date	Text	Icons
	Example	
	Example	
	Example	
	Example	

If you want to change all the found items, you can simply click on Replace All   Ctrl+Shift+R in the Action Menu:

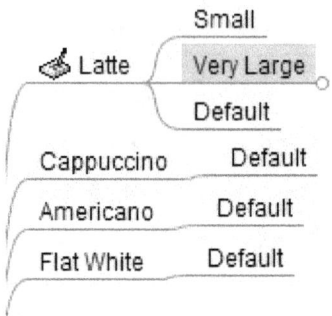

If you want to replace only selected nodes you can move the mouse down to the results and click on the text for the node you want to replace all the text for and click it to select the row:

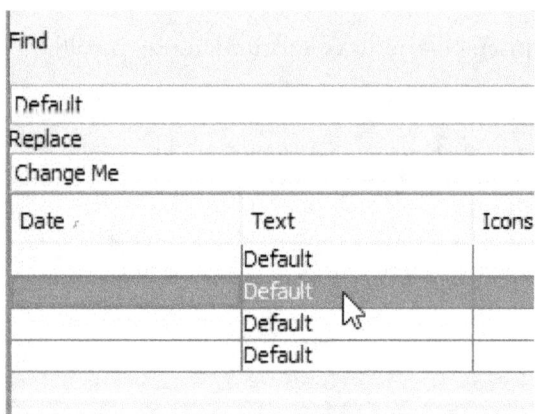

Then hit Select Ctrl+S to select the Node in the Mind Map:

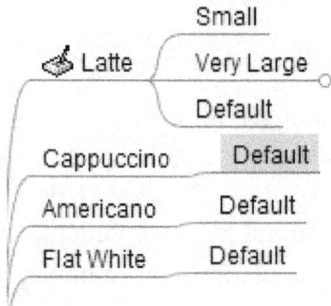

And Replace Selected   Ctrl+R   in the Action menu to replace the entire selected node:

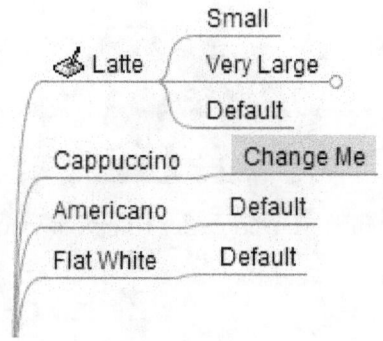

Click on Cancel   Escape   in the Action menu to close the Find and Replace dialogue.

Blinking Nodes

While making a node blink can irritate some people it is definitely useful when you want to draw someone's attention. To make a node blink select the node, then click on
⃝⃝ Blinking Node   in the Format menu.

The node will keep on changing colours until you develop a migraine, select the node and click on ⃝⃝ Blinking Node   in the Format menu to turn it back off again.

This feature isn't exactly recommended.

Images

While a plain old text mind map can look pretty good, it's often nice to add images to the mind map. For example, we might want to add the following image

To an existing Mind Map in order to give a visual clue about the topic.

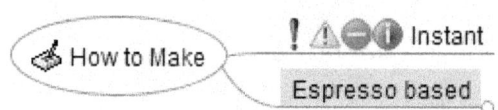

First, select the node where you want to add the image. Then click on   Image (File Chooser or Link)...   Alt+K   in the Insert Menu.

This will open a File Open dialogue.

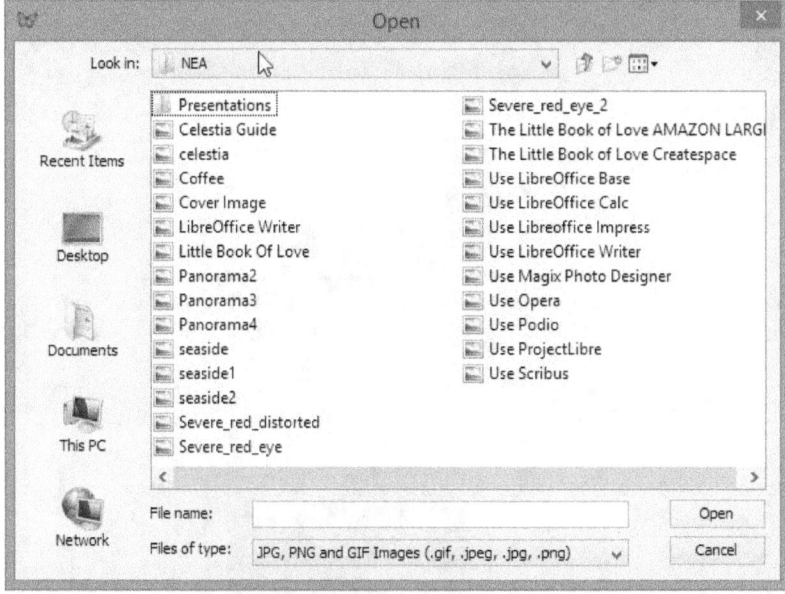

Select the Folder in the normal way.

Then double click on the file name that you want to open.

You'll lose the text under the node, as below.

Click on the node to select it, then

Edit Node   F2   in the Edit menu to open the Node Editor. You'll notice that the only thing in it is an Image.

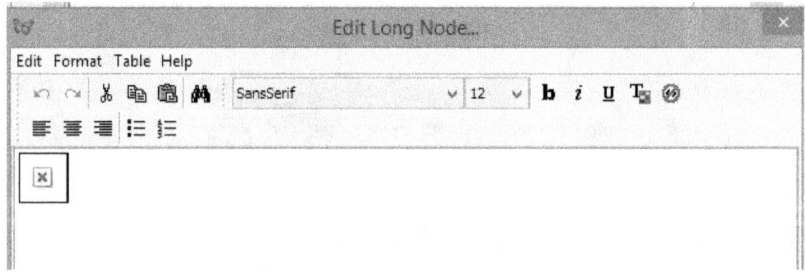

Add text to the node by clicking after the node, pressing enter, then entering the text:

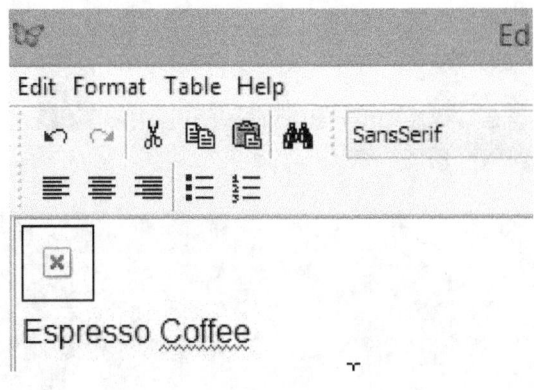

Then click OK .

You'll find that images really enhance a mind map but it's important to make sure that you don't add too many – you want the mind map to be small enough so you take it in all at once.

Scaling an Image

Sometimes an Image is simply too large on the screen. This causes a problem since FreeMind doesn't have an Image editor. You have to scale it using third party software program. While you can use any program to do this, there is a program provided by Microsoft that can do it for you.

Click on [window icon] to open the start page then [search icon] to search. Type Paint into the box.

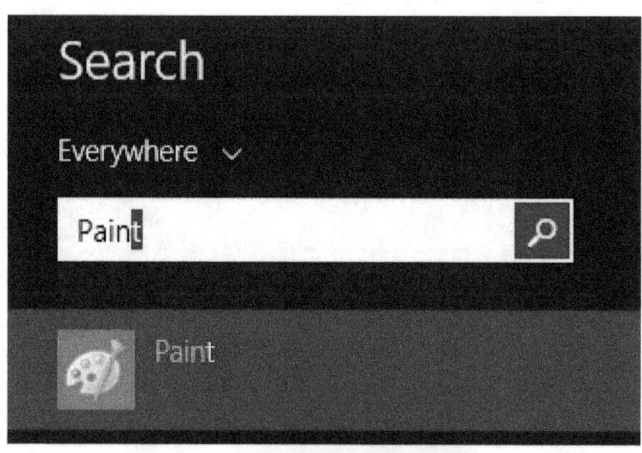

Click on the Paint Logo [Paint logo image] to open Microsoft Paint.

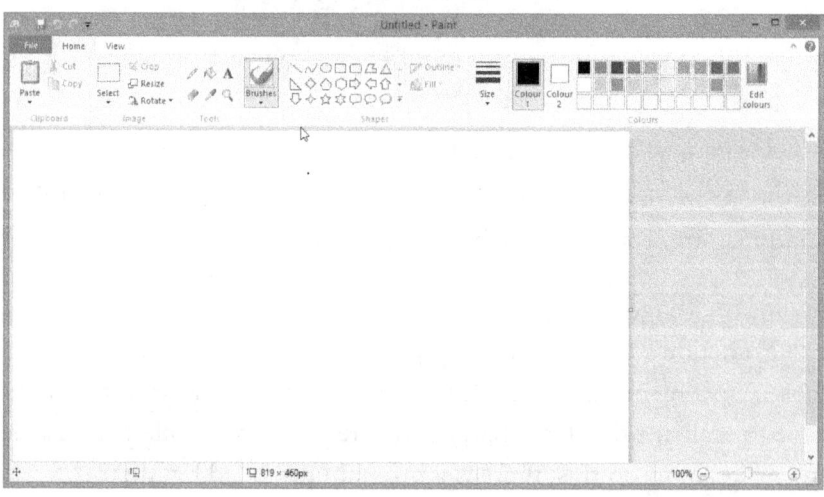

Open the Image

Click on 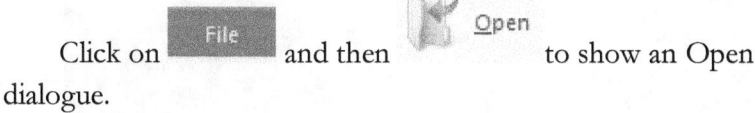 and then to show an Open dialogue.

Choose the directory from the directory list on the left hand side of the screen:

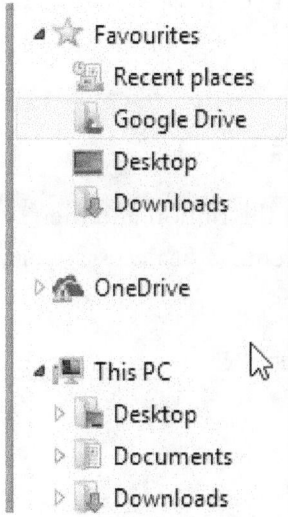

Then click to show a preview, and select the file you want to edit from the list.

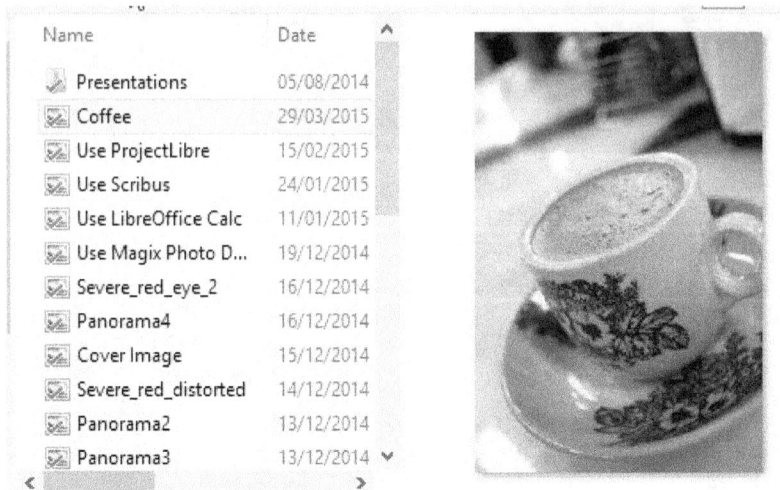

If you're happy that you're opening the right file click on **Open** .

Resizing the File

Click on Home in the ribbon and then Resize . Make sure you are resizing by percentage (if necessary click on the round circle to the left By: ◯ Percentage so the dialogue shows the following:

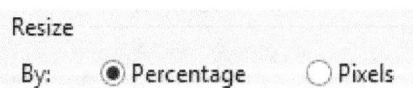

Make sure that you maintain the aspect ratio ✔ Maintain aspect ratio this means that you're reducing the width and the height by the same amount. You don't want the image to end up looking strange.

Now it's just a case of deciding what percentage to scale the drawing by.

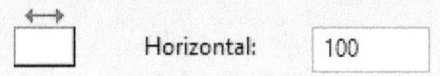

100% means it's the original size, 25% means it's a quarter of the size, 200% would make it double the size. If you make it larger you may lose quality so I don't recommend doing it.

Click 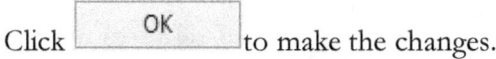 to make the changes.

You can see a preview of the image in the main viewable are of Paint.

If you're not happy click on ▓ next to the ▓ at the top of the screen. This will undo the changes that you've made.

Saving As

Once you're happy with the changes I recommend saving them as a different file name. This means that you will not lose the original image. Click on  and then .

This will display a Save as dialogue. Make sure you select the right directory, and change the File Name to a new name.

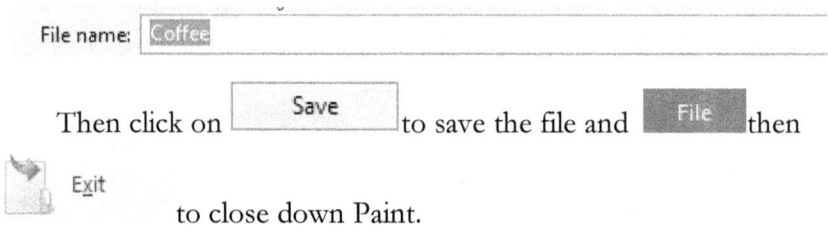

Then click on Save to save the file and File then

Exit to close down Paint.

Now you've scaled the image you can insert it into the Mind Map without it taking up too much space!

Zooming in or Out of the Mind Map

Sometimes when you have a large Mind Map you may want to zoom out to allow you to see it all in one go. In the toolbar click on the Zoom combo box which is to the left of the Font box:

This will provide you with a list of different zoom amounts:

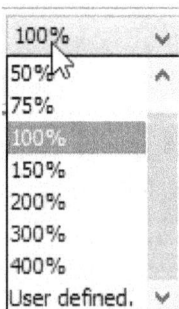

They more or less operate as you'd expect them to. For example 50% means that your image will be half size:

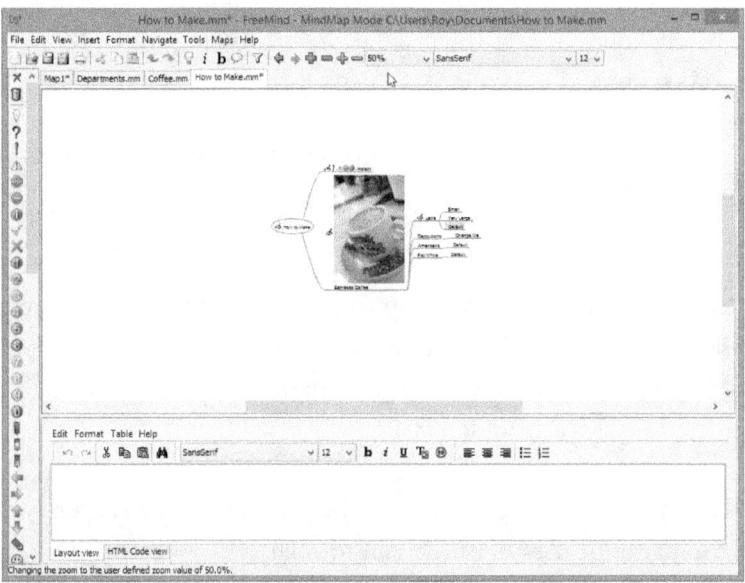

And 200% means it will be double size:

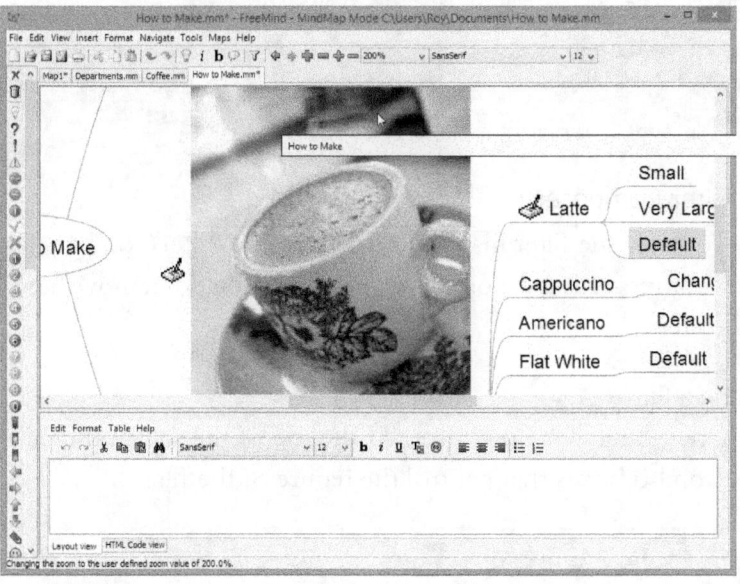

Moving Forward or Back in the Mind Map

You can move Back a node by clicking on ⬅ in the taskbar or by pressing ALT+Left on the keyboard. You can move Forward a node by clicking on ⇨ in the taskbar or by pressing ALT+Right on the Keyboard.

Pressing the Escape key (Esc on the keyboard) moves directly to the Root Node.

Filtering Mind Map

You can Filter the Mind Map to show nodes that only contain specific text or icons. This can be useful when you are using a large mind map so that you only see Nodes that have properties like Completed tasks, or troubled tasks.

To turn on Filtering click ▽ in the toolbar. You'll see a new filter toolbar appear under the main toolbar:

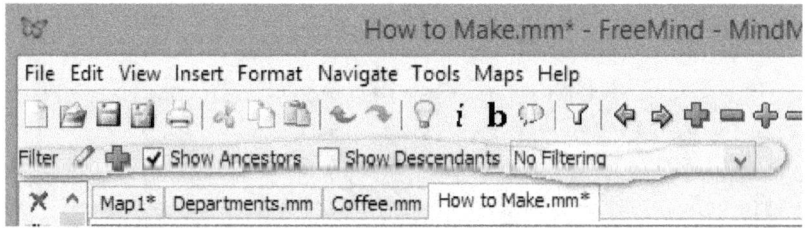

The Filter Composer

To show the filter manager click ✎ in the Filter Toolbar. The Filter Composer is a dialog that you can use to add, remove, and apply filters.

Adding a Filter

Open the Filter Composer. At the top of the screen there are three combo boxes that control the nature of the filter.

1. **The Restraint Type Box**
2. **The Constraint Box**
3. **The Search Box**

Click on the Restraint Type box to choose whether to make a filter based on the Node Text or the Icon.

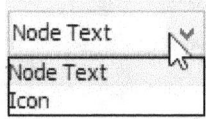

Then on the Constraint Box to choose whether the Node will contain or NOT contain the content of the Search Box.

Finally, if you're editing text type it into the Search Box. If your filter is based on Icons, click on the box and select the icon to filter:

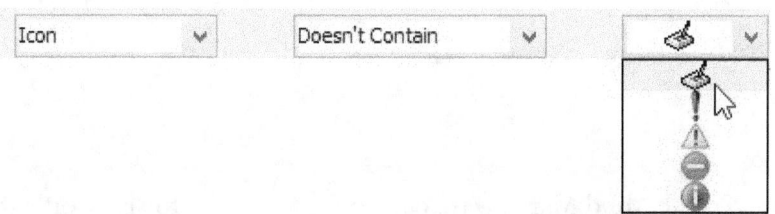

Filters nodes based on whether they don't contain a Note.

Filters nodes based on whether they contain the text "Default". By default the Filter is case sensitive ("As" is not the same word as "as") if you want FreeMind to ignore the case when determining if a node matches the criteria click the rectangle round ).

Press Add to Add a filter to the list.

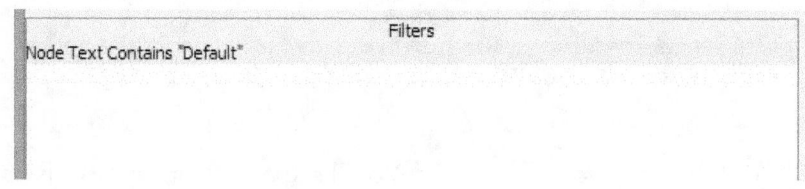

Applying a Filter

Say you have the following Mind Map:

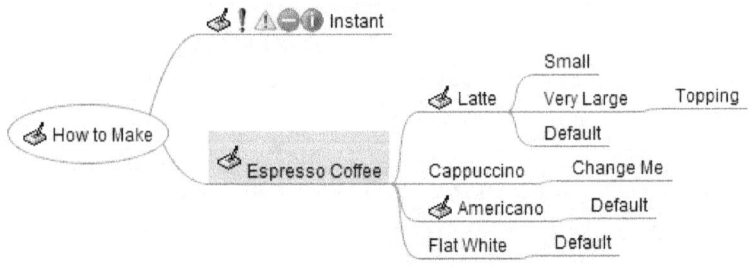

And you want to Apply the constraint:

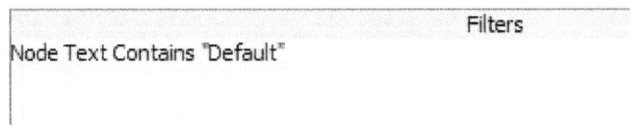

To the Mind Map, please click on **Apply** to show only the Nodes that match the Filter.

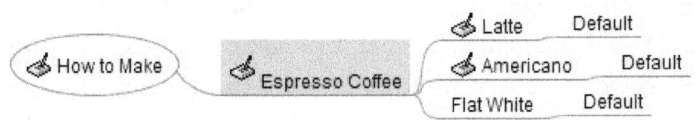

Reversing the Meaning of a Filter

To reverse the meaning of a filter click on the filter in the List.

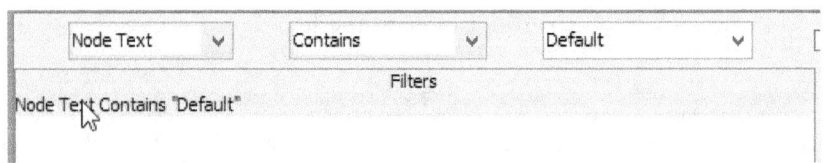

And then click on **Not**. You'll see two filters appear in the Filters List:

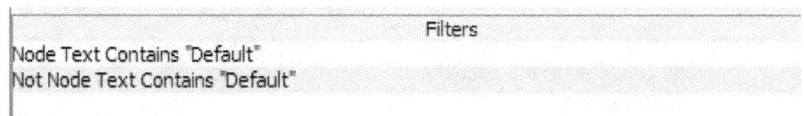

Select the filter that you want to apply by clicking on it, and then click Apply . For example:

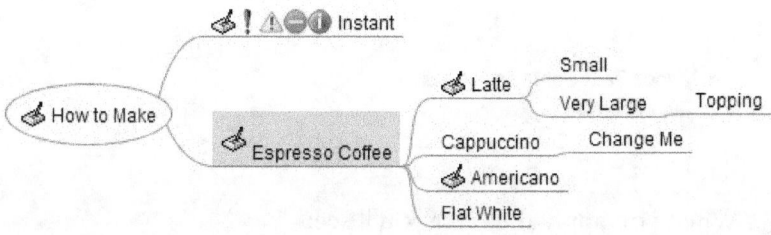

Will result in the following:

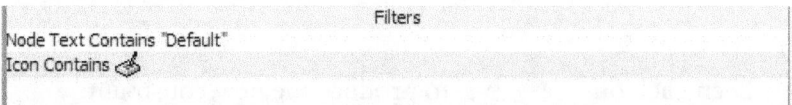

Using More than One Filter at a Time

You'll sometimes want to do a slightly more complicated Filter where two conditions are considered at the same time. There are two such conditions: AND and OR.

AND means that for a filter to be batched both the first filter and the second filter must be matched.

OR means that either the first or second filter can be true.

And

Say that we have the following two filters that we've added:

We want to do a filter for all Nodes that contain Default and have a Note.

Select both conditions by clicking on the first, then holding shift down and clicking on the second (and keep shift down to add any other conditions you want to filter. Let go when you've finished adding filters).

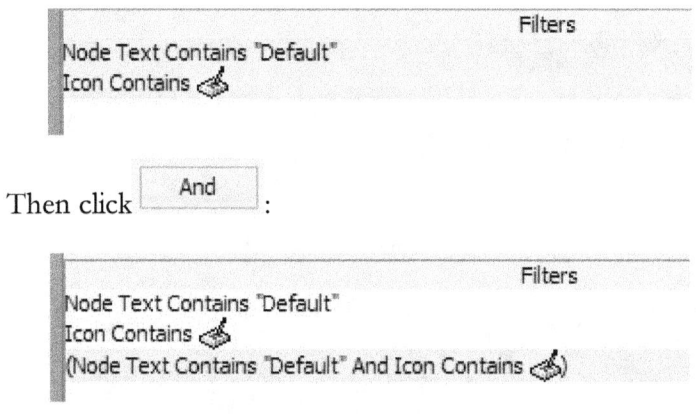

Then click [And] :

When you apply the filter you'll see:

Or

When you want a filter to match any of two or more sets of conditions use or.

Select the filters you want using the method in the section above:

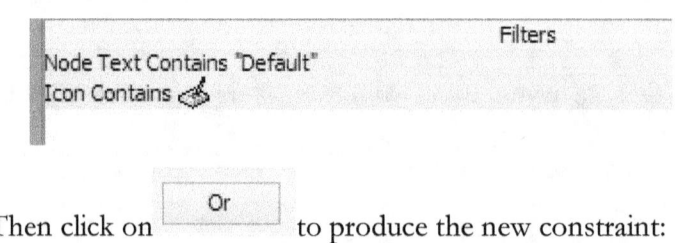

Then click on [Or] to produce the new constraint:

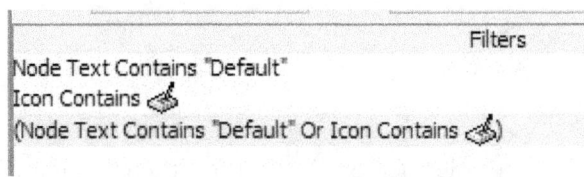

When you apply the Filter you'll see:

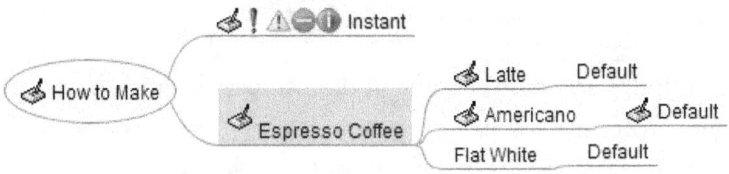

Removing a Filter from the List

To remove a Filter from the list first select it by clicking on it:

Filters
Node Text Contains "Default"
Icon Contains 🧹
(Node Text Contains "Default" Or Icon Contains 🧹)

And then press Delete .

Saving Filters

It can take a while to get your filters just the way you want them. Saving a filter list can save substantial time.

Click on Save to show a save as dialogue. Choose the directory that you want to save the file to.

Save in: 📄 Documents ⌄

And then the FileName:

File name: |

And then Click [Save].

Loading Filters

To load a filter file click on [Load] then change the directory to the one where you saved the file.

| Look in: | 📄 Documents | ⌄ |

And double click on the File in the list just like any other Open Dialogue. Note that when you open a file you'll overwrite your existing filter selections so it's important to save any filters that you don't want to lose.

Closing Filter Composer

If you want to apply a filter and then close the filter composer select the filter from the list and click [OK]. If you just want to close the filter composer without applying any new filter click [Cancel].

Filter Toolbar

While you use the Filter composer to create filters, and can use it to apply them as well, you'll often find yourself applying filters from the Filter Toolbar. In addition, the Filter Toolbar can be used to control the effect of filters on Branches.

Applying a Filter

To apply a filter click on the Filter combo box in the Filters Toolbar. This is the box after show descendants.

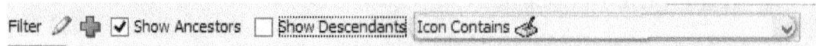

Clicking it will show a list of the filters that you've already created using the Filter Composer.

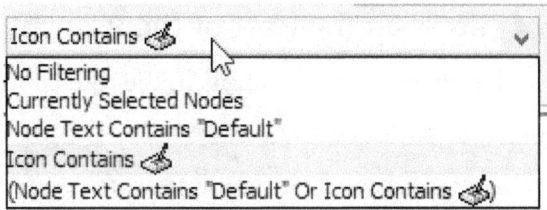

Clicking on No Filtering will show the entire Mind map:

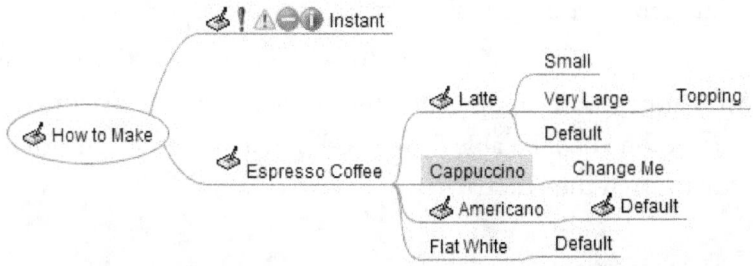

Choosing Currently Selected Nodes will filter based on the nodes you've currently selected:

This may not seem particularly useful, but depending on how you change the show Ancestors and Show Descendants properties you can use it to filter out particular branches:

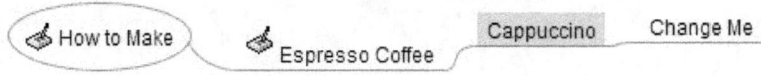

Finally, you can apply any of the filters that you've already created by clicking on them.

Effect of Filters on the Rest of the Branch

You'll see that there are two options in the toolbar that we haven't come to yet ✔ Show Ancestors ✔ Show Descendants . The Filter selects nodes that correspond to its conditions (for example

Currently Selected Nodes ⌄ Filters the Mind map based on currently selected nodes).

While the Root node is always show no matter what Filter is applied, turning off ✔ Show Ancestors by clicking on the ✔ will mean that Ancestor (parent) nodes along the entire branch aren't displayed. If it's turned on you'll be able to see nodes that are the parents of nodes that match the criteria:

Filter ✏ ➕ ✔ Show Ancestors ☐ Show Descendants Node Text Contains "Default" ⌄

Will show:

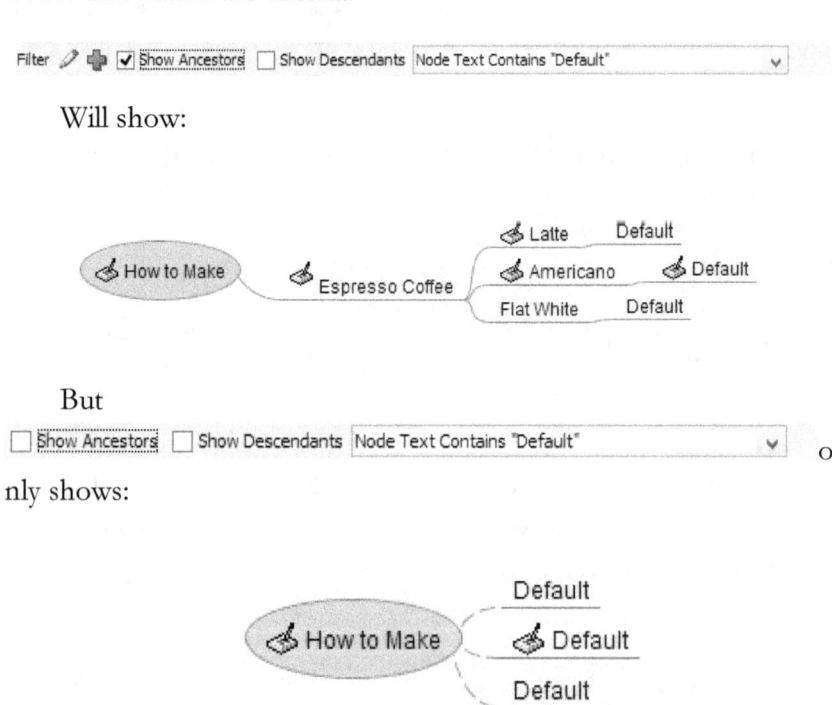

But

☐ Show Ancestors ☐ Show Descendants Node Text Contains "Default" ⌄ o

nly shows:

Descendants will include nodes that are child nodes of those nodes that match the criteria.

Filter 🖉 ➕ ☐ Show Ancestors ☐ Show Descendants Icon Contains 🖌

Displays:

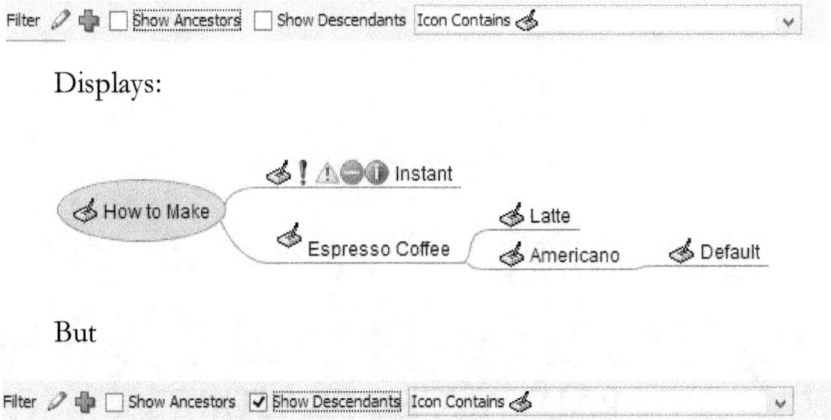

But

Filter 🖉 ➕ ☐ Show Ancestors ☑ Show Descendants Icon Contains 🖌

Will display the entire mind map since the root note contains 🖌 .

Next Chapter

In this chapter I've tried to give you more information on how to Edit a mind map.

The next chapter will include information about Advanced features that Free Mind has that can be used to link to other document, schedule tasks and handle dates, and automatically format a mind map.

4 ADVANCED FEATURES

At this point we've made a mind map, saved it, and changed its appearance to make it look great. We've also learned how to add notes to nodes.

This chapter covers advanced features that FreeMind provides to browse the file hierarchy, link to other documents or mind maps and schedule tasks. While you can create a great mind map with the information you've already learned in the book this section will provide you with some extra bonus functionality that can be very useful.

File Mode Map

If you click   File Mode   Alt+3   in the Maps menu you'll see a Mind Map of the directory structure of your computer:

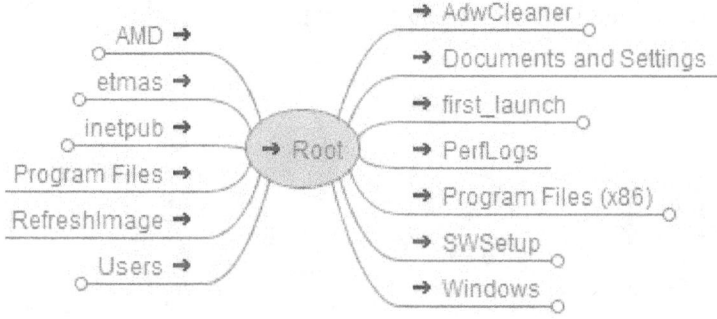

Each of these nodes corresponds to a directory off the main root drive. Expanding these nodes will either show files (which when you click them will open) or further directories.

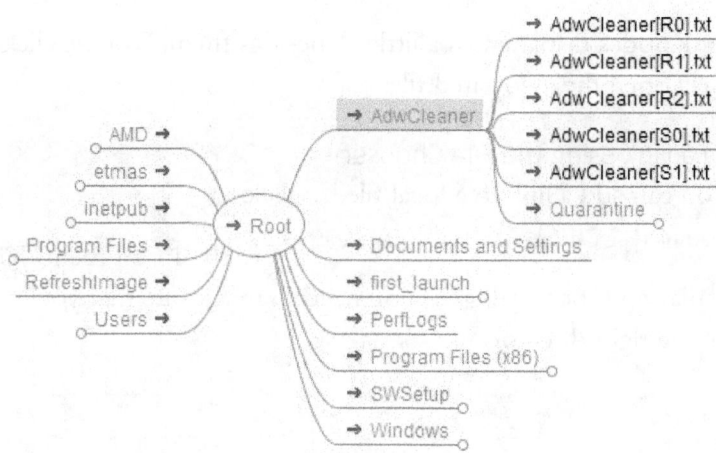

Double clicking on a node will open the associated File or Directory.

Automatic Formatting

Sometimes you might want to make a Mind Map pretty without actually spending very much time or effort formatting the Mind Map yourself. FreeMind has an option 🔧 Automatic Layout in the Format menu that provides some basic formatting for you which does improve the look of a basic Mind Map:

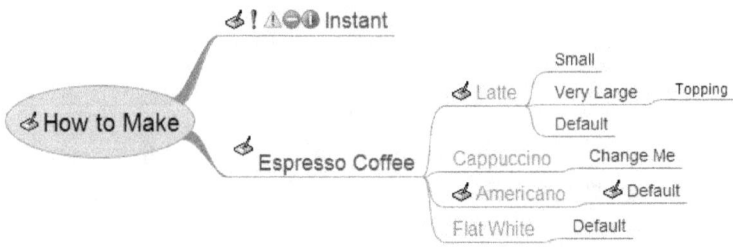

Links

We've seen links previously. A link is very similar to a hyperlink in a web page. It allows you to open a file or another program. There were links in the previous section on the File Map.

Link nodes display with a little → besides them. Double clicking them will open the associated file.

Adding a Link using the File Chooser

You can add a link to a local file by clicking on Hyperlink (File Chooser)...   Ctrl+Shift+K   in the Insert menu. This will display an Open dialogue. You need to make sure that you choose the right directory.

Then double click on the file that you want to link to when someone double clicks on the Node. The file will be opened by the default program for that file type which means that a Mind Map will be opened by Free Mind.

Manually Editing a Link

You can edit a link by selecting its' node, and then clicking Hyperlink (Text Field)...   Ctrl+K   in the Insert Menu.

There are two things to notice about this. The first is the odd %20 thing in the text. FreeMind interprets a space as %20, so the link is "Types Of Coffee.mm" to a human being. When you type in a filename use %20 instead of the space bar. E.g.

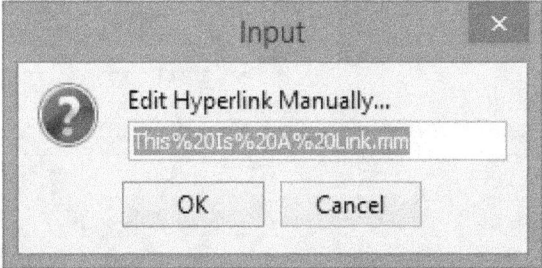

The second thing to note is that these links are relative. You can link to a file in another directory. If you have ../ before the file name it looks up one directory. If you have a directory name and then /it means look in that directory:

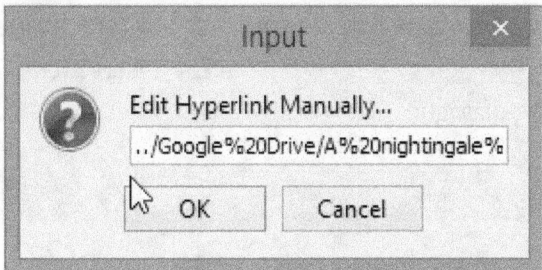

Means starting in the current files directory go up one and then into the Google Drive directory and choose a file from that directory

I don't really recommend manually editing links unless you are linking to a web page (see below) because I find the file picker to be much more easy to use and useful.

Link to a Webpage

Create a link to a web page selecting its node, and then clicking Hyperlink (Text Field)...   Ctrl+K in the Insert Menu. Then type in the web page's URL or web address:

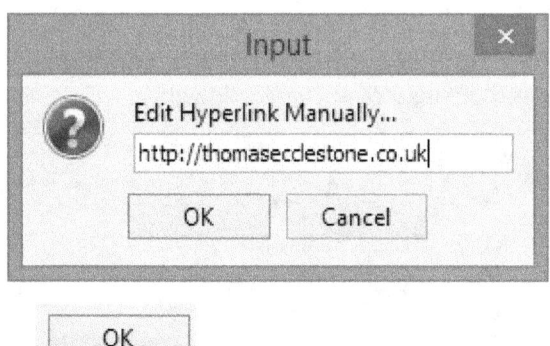

And press 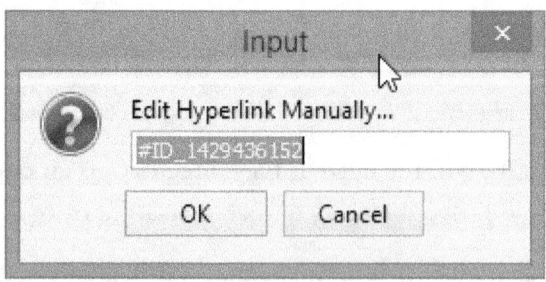 .

When you double click on the link the internet browser will open automatically to show you the web page.

Removing a Link

Select a node with a link that you want to remove, then click Hyperlink (Text Field)...   Ctrl+K in the Insert Menu. This will show an Input dialogue.

Double click on the text in the Edit Hyperlink Manually box and delete it. Then press [OK] . The Mind Map will be deleted automatically.

Calendar and Dates

It's often useful to be able to schedule a node for action of some kind. For example, if you have a diagram with the following nodes:

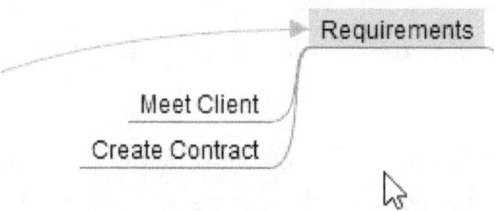

You may want to add a date to the node "Meet Client". You can do this through the Calendar tool. First select the node that you want to add a date to. Click on Show Calendar...   Ctrl+T in the Tools Menu. This will show you a Calendar with the current date highlighted in red.

Time Management							✕
Actions							
March					2015		
	Mon	Tue	Wed	Thu	Fri	Sat	Sun
09							1
10	2	3	4	5	6	7	8
11	9	10	11	12	13	14	15
12	16	17	18	19	20	21	22
13	23	24	25	26	27	28	29
14	30	31					

Going to next Month and last Month.

There are three months shown at any one time. The currently selected day will be in the middle calendar. At first it will be today's date:

Note that the currently selected date is a grey square. Today's date is in red.

The first calendar on the screen is the previous month, and the last calendar is the next month. If you select a day in the next month by clicking on it the calendar layout will change so that the month is displayed in the centre.

However, you don't have to scroll through the months to get to the correct one. Notice that above the currently selected day is a combo box with month and a text field with year.

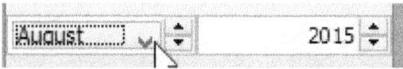

Click on the combo box to display a list of months to choose from:

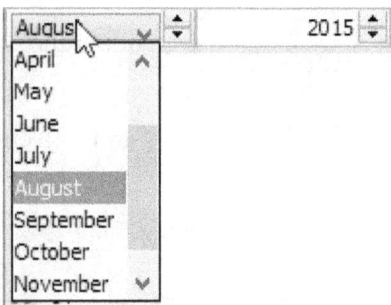

And change the year field to the correct year by typing into it.

For example,  is June 2022.

Going to Today

It is often useful to go to the current day without having to scroll through the calendars or change the date using the combo box. Click on Today   Home in the Action menu to go to Today in the calendar.

Append Date to Selected Node

There are two ways to use the Calendar. The first is simply to append a date and/or time to the end of a node. This just adds it as text to the node. You could remove the date by editing the node in the normal way. The second is as a Reminder which I will explain latter on.

Select the node that you want to append the date to. Then open the Calendar if you don't already have it open by clicking on Show Calendar...   Ctrl+T in the Tools Menu. Then, click on the date if it's shown in the calendar to select it or alternatively change the month and year and then click on the date.

Once your date is selecting it, appending the date to the end of the Node is easy. Just click on Append Date To Selected Nodes   F2   in the Action menu.

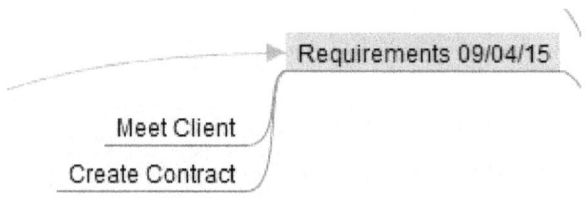

Note that you can edit the node in the normal way (double click on it, or right click and choose Edit Node   F2 in the context sensitive menu then just delete the appended date in the normal way:

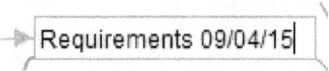

Create New Node with Date

Make sure you have a node selected, then choose the date in the calendar and click on Create new node with the date   Ctrl+N to make a child node with the date you have selected.

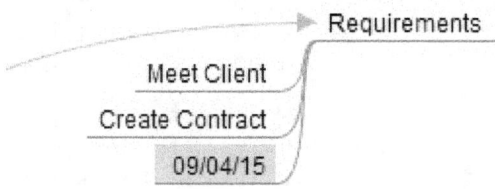

You can edit the node by selecting it and clicking | Edit Node | F2 |.

Create New Sibling Node with Date

Make sure you have a node selected, then choose the date in the calendar and click on

Create new sibling node with the date Enter in the Edit menu.

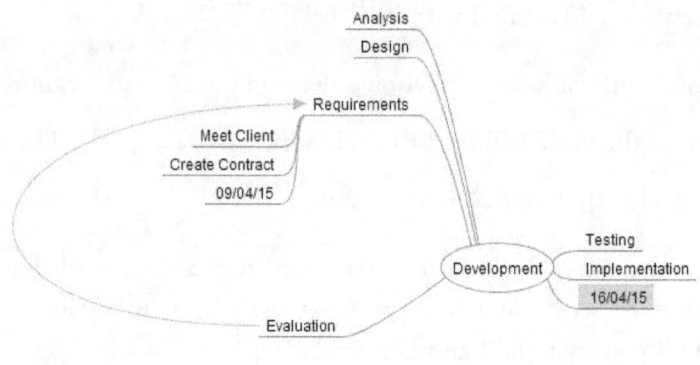

Reminder

While it is sometimes useful to append a date using text the main use of the Calendar is probably to set reminders. This provides a visual clue that an important date has passed. Select the node which has a task that you want to be reminded about. Then show the calendar, and choose the date.

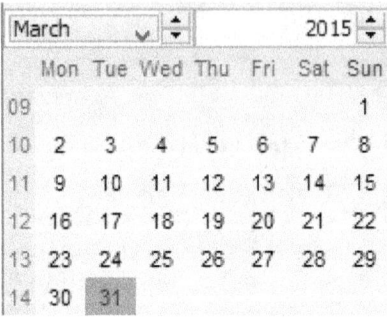

The thing that you need to remember about reminders is you also have a time attached to them. Below all the Calendars is a time in the 24 hour clock. For example Hour: 14 Minute: 45 is quarter to three in the afternoon.

When you've selected a date and a time, click on Remind Me At This Date   Ctrl+R . You'll see the node has a new icon associated with it: Requirements ⊘ .

FreeMind will wait until you've reached the reminder point and the icon in the node will start to flash between ⊘ and 🔔 . The root node will also flash between a ↖ and ⊘ icon.

Unfortunately the current version of FreeMind can only have one reminder per node. It will prompt you with the following warning if you try to add another reminder:

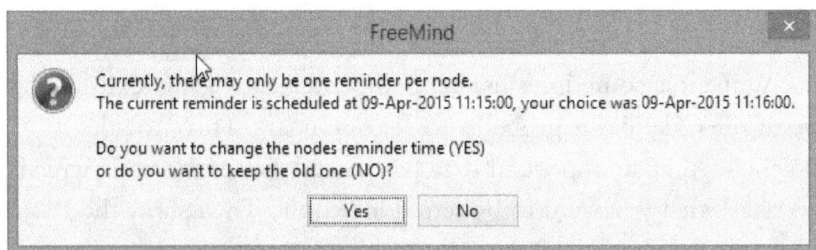

Click Yes to change the reminder time, and No to keep the old one.

Remove Reminder

You can remove a Reminder from a node by selecting the node, then opening the calendar and

clicking Remove Reminder   Backspace .

Time Scheduler

The Time scheduler allows you search nodes with reminders. Click on Show Time Scheduler List... in the Tools menu to show the Time Scheduler.

You can search for specific node text using the Find box:

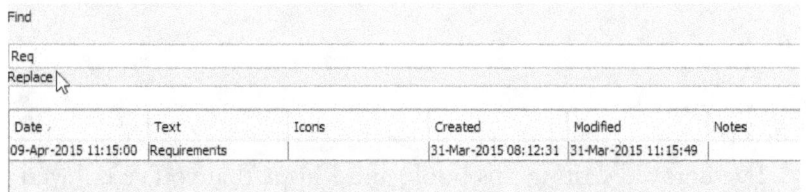

And then double click on the node that you want to go to. Opening the Calendar and Time Scheduler at the same time can be very useful. Move the windows so they are side by side:

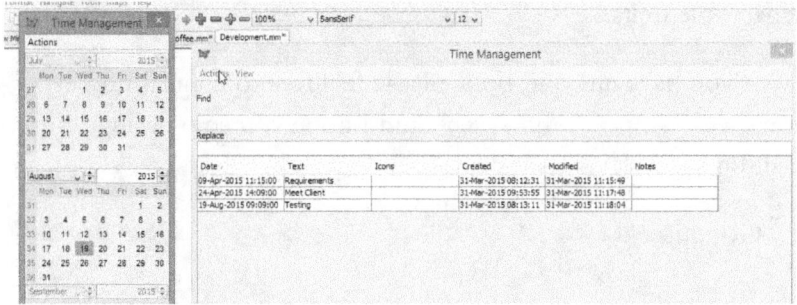

In the Time Scheduler search for the node, and then single click on the one that you want to change the time for to select it:

Date	Text	Icons	Created	Modified	Notes
09-Apr-2015 11:15:00	Requirements		31-Mar-2015 08:12:31	31-Mar-2015 11:15:49	
24-Apr-2015 14:09:00	Meet Client		31-Mar-2015 09:53:55	31-Mar-2015 11:17:48	
19-Aug-2015 09:09:00	Testing		31-Mar-2015 08:13:11	31-Mar-2015 11:18:04	

Then hit Select Ctrl+S in the Time Schedulers
Action menu.

Now, make your changes to the node in the Calendar window,
for example removing the Reminder using

Remove Reminder Backspace in the Calendars Action
menu.

Thanks!

I've enjoyed writing this book, and I hope that you've enjoyed
reading it. By now you should have learned how to create, format,
export and edit Mind Maps. We've covered most of the features of
FreeMind which are useful when you want to produce
documentation, work on projects, and break down tasks into
manageable units.

If you have any questions please feel free to contact me on
thomasecclestone@yahoo.co.uk and I hope you enjoy using
FreeMind!

Good Luck!

ABOUT THE AUTHOR

Thomas Ecclestone is a software engineer and technical writer who lives in Kent, England. After getting his 1st class honours in software engineering he worked at the National Computing Centre in Manchester, the Manchester Metropolitan University, and for BEC systems Integration before starting his own business in software development. He is a writer who lives on a smallholding in Kent where he looks after a small flock of Hebridean sheep.